ONE TO GROW ON

LEARN IT. LIVE IT. LOVE IT!

ONE TO GROW ON

LEARN IT. LIVE IT. LOVE IT!

KEVIN M. WAUGAMAN

Copyright © 2024
Kevin M. Waugaman

Performance Publishing
McKinney, TX

All Worldwide Rights Reserved.

All rights reserved. No part of this publication may be reproduced, stored in a retrieval system or transmitted, in any form or by any means, electronic, mechanical, recorded, photocopied, or otherwise, without the prior written permission of the copyright owner, except by a reviewer who may quote brief passages in a review.

ISBN: 978-1-961781-32-0 (paperback)

Edited by Christina Boys
CEB Editorial Services
www.cebeditorial.com

For Jessica, Elliott, and Raelynn. My love for each of you strengthens every day.

Elliott, when I asked for your contribution to this book when you were 3 years old, you answered perfectly: "It is important to push in chairs when you get up from the table."

CONTENTS

Introduction ix

Beliefs and Values
First Comes Forgiveness 3
Get Clear On Your Mission/Vision/Principles (M.V.P.) 13
Family Matters 25
Flock With the Right Crew 35
Joy In Simple Things 47
Fear Is the Biggest Liar 57

Habits and Results
Winning the Day 71
Powerful Programming 85
Right Actions Lead to Strong Results 99
Ideas Are Cheap, Execution Is Gold 107
Your Best Today Will Set Up Your Best Tomorrow 117
Grow Your Sales Ability, Grow Your Influence 125

Challenges and Solutions
Develop a Calmness to Your Style 147
Opportunity Cost and The Credit Card Crisis 159
Challenges Indicate Progress 171

Your Income Is Equal to Your Ability to Solve Problems.............181
The Power of Creating Options..195

Get It Done
Routines, Not Ruts 209

Conclusion..217
Appendices...221

INTRODUCTION

WHY YOU SHOUD READ THIS BOOK

This book is designed to be a starting point for your personal growth journey. It may serve as preparation for entering the real world, or it may assist you in adjusting your current life approach. No matter what stage of life you're in, chances are you are going through an awakening of sorts if you're reading these words. I've been there. You might find yourself wishing to make the transition from some of your more childish behaviors into "adulting." Notice I say *some* childish behaviors, for there are some behaviors you will want to hang on to and never give up.

There are thousands of books, podcasts, and essays touching on personal growth, self-help, business, sales, and different mindsets to adopt, and I've read quite a few of them. There is so much in the way of advice and guidance out there. And that is why I endeavored to write a book that is:

1. Easy to digest and apply while staying true to your personality
2. Fun to read
3. Filled with possible action steps for immediate use

4. Supportive of trusted relationships and good values
5. A trove of resources for anyone seeking to dive deeper in a particular subject

My goal is to impact your life in a positive way, whether it be a minor improvement or a major shift. (Here's a secret: Major shifts generally come as a result of minor improvements over time.)

The challenge is for you to show up, be present when you read this, and act on the to-dos. In each chapter, there is a list of ideas to implement what was discussed. If you take action along the way, you will start to notice big differences. My hope is that this return on investment will take form in both a higher quality of life and finances, if that is your desire. The return on just reading the book might be good, but if you take action as a result, the return will be hundreds of times greater over time.

I want to help you avoid some of the mistakes I have made while also imparting an understanding that making mistakes in life is a necessity. You see, it is difficult to admit that I have regrets. Life has been challenging, but the journey has been great for me overall. I was blessed with great parents and extended family, a loving wife, and kids I cherish.

But prior to any success, there was a period of intense brokenness. See, my life could have gone in an entirely different direction if I had let it. It took my faith, lots of books and podcasts, introspection, and great mentors to help get me on the right path. Mom and Dad were great, too, as they each in their own way instilled values in me. But I was a bit of a rebel and needed some outside influence as well.

The adversity that I have overcome isn't as dramatic as some stories you'll hear. Growing up, we moved around a lot. The east coast of Florida is pretty familiar to me, all the way from Islamorada to Jacksonville. There were challenges, for sure: my parents' divorce, big family riffs, untimely and tragic deaths of family and friends, getting laid off, a major financial crisis, health scares, overeating, overworking, over-partying. But over the years, I woke up and changed my mindset. I started taking more intentional positive action. Thankfully, all of this eventually progressed into a level of harmony in life that, while never perfect, is certainly a major improvement over where I was headed. Without taking action and working on my mindset in the way outlined in this book, my current scenario would be awful. And please hear me and believe me on this: We can all get a little better each day.

So, where are you in your life? Is there something that you are dealing with that is way off? Or are you oblivious to the God-given power we have in our minds and bodies to create an amazing life (as I was for most of my 20s and even into my 30s)?

Life is not perfect. I am not perfect—far from it, in fact. Whenever I feel like I'm giving myself too much credit for something, I utter the words Nicole Kidman told Tom Cruise in *Days of Thunder*: "Control is an illusion, you infantile egomaniac!" And of course, I do so in a feminine British accent to really nail the impression.

Results do matter, though, which is why I thought it would lend some credibility to the words contained within these pages, words that share what has changed for me throughout my journey. Some of these transitions have already taken place, while others are still works in progress:

- Deep in debt *to* financial freedom
- Relationally challenged *to* married to my beautiful wife

- Childhood *to* fatherhood (this was a major struggle)
- Party animal *to* moderate alcohol consumption
- Chain smoker *to* non-smoker
- Ego-driven *to* service-driven
- Blamer *to* forgiver
- Blood pressure improved from 160/100 *to* 125/75
- Dropped weight from 220 pounds *to* 195 (with occasional gusts up to 200)
- Talker *to* listener (although, I can talk)
- Pessimist *to* optimist *to* possibilist
- Short-tempered *to* compassionate
- From last in sales at one company *to* second by my third year (then moved into a leadership role)
- Rookie leader *to* consistent Chairman's Cup dynasty run for an office I led
- Entry-level employee *to* CEO of a 550-person organization consisting of real estate agents and employees
- Hobby writer *to* writing and publishing a book with the goal of positively impacting millions of lives
- Corporate staffer *to* founder of a company with a mission to help people maximize potential and remove dream barriers
- Most importantly, a sinner who found a Savior (still a sinner sometimes—we all are)

I would also be remiss to minimize the value of the relationships borne from my days of struggle. I have friends to this day that I wouldn't trade for anything, and many of those friendships blossomed during my late teens and early twenties, when much of my life was aimless. (Not worthless, but certainly aimless.) Many of the characteristics and traits I eventually developed were present within, but I hadn't started cultivating them until a bit later than I would have liked.

The point is not to try and avoid all struggle. That isn't possible. The point is to develop a higher awareness of:

1. Your mindset
2. Your purpose
3. What matters most to you
4. How you can proactively live a life of success, significance, and contribution

I hope this book launches you into further study and action on the four areas listed above. There are plenty of books I recommend that can keep you busy for a while and, hopefully, fully engaged in creating a better life. Currently, I am mainly focused on #4: living a life of significance and contribution. What I mean by this is that I am taking a more outward approach to positively influencing others. I now aim to impact others' lives on a larger scale than what I previously delivered in my career and personal life.

I wrote this book with my son Elliott and daughter Raelynn in mind. I love them deeply and want to preserve some of the life lessons I've picked up along the way—with the hopes that they might gain some insight and understanding earlier in life than I did. I hope the passages in this book are helpful for you, too, and one of the best investments in time you will ever make.

IF YOU WANT TO DIVE DEEPER INTO THIS JOURNEY AND LEARN MORE ABOUT OUR PERSONAL DEVELOPMENT PROGRAM, PLEASE VISIT https://momentorsllc.com/one-to-grow-on-community/.

BELIEFS AND VALUES

FIRST COMES FORGIVENESS

Your growth may depend on it

What are you carrying around with you? You are unique, and you are a person of value. I know this to be true. Sure, you also have some baggage, but so does everyone! You are reading or listening to this book because personal growth is important to you. Often, before a transformation can occur, we need to let go of past transgressions or traumas. We must forgive others for our traumas and forgive ourselves for transgressions. We must also ask for forgiveness when appropriate. I am neither a psychologist nor a pastor, so the process of forgiveness may require talking to a professional if your past is riddled with trauma. It is very difficult for some to move forward until their heavy burdens are addressed. But when we do deal with our trauma, we can move forward with a lighter load.

I know this, too: Life is too short to allow the past to penetrate our lives and perpetuate negativity and fear.

I often see people blaming others for their circumstances. There is so much anger and resentment everywhere. I see disagreements that unnecessarily escalate past the point of no return. I know people who are holding long-term grudges, walking around with a poisonous attitude because of something that happened days, weeks, months, or even *years* ago! I see people who are so afraid of hurting others' feelings or having their feelings hurt. What are we doing?

Of course, I am not advocating for hurting others' feelings, nor am I minimizing major past events that people are trying to work through. What I *am* suggesting is that you *address* these things. Get help! Don't let someone else's baggage dominate your life. I am also advocating for not taking ourselves too seriously with the minor stuff we face along the way. If you believe you were wronged by someone, and you carry that around with you, well, guess what? The person that wronged you occupies space rent-free in your brain, which affects how you live your life and interact with others. In that sense, you have completely empowered them! That's right: You get to make that choice. People cannot make you feel anything—you must choose the emotion. Call me old-fashioned, but the antidote for so much of what we struggle with today is often good communication. (More on that later.)

Speaking of offensive, I hope some of the context in this chapter doesn't rub you the wrong way. It would be less than authentic for me to share ideas on forgiveness without also mentioning my faith. Faith improved my ability to truly forgive and believe that I am forgiven. It is a core tenet of Christianity. If you are not a person of faith, that is completely okay. I value you as a human being no matter what you believe in. And I am hopeful that this book can help you multiply that value internally and for others.

Many successful people I know believe in something bigger—something spiritual in nature. The content within these pages is

ONE TO GROWN ON

based on my Christian values. This book very well may put you on the path to achieving your wildest dreams and accomplishing all you set your mind to. What it is *not* designed to do, however, is make you believe you are the master of the universe. The wisdom set forth in this book and the hundreds of other books I have read comes directly from God. The most important thing, to me, is that this context is from God, and therefore God deserves the credit, the gratitude, and the best of all of us. In terms of our mindset and belief systems, there is no substitute for the Almighty. If you start to think that you are the creator of all things good in your life, I encourage you to put this book down and pick up THE book.

As I mentioned, forgiveness is key to joy and success. One thing many of us need to do is forgive our past selves for how we treated both ourselves and others. For instance, I treated my body poorly in my 20s and 30s and even put others at risk along the way. But guess what? I am not the person I was 20 years ago, 20 months ago, 20 weeks ago, or even 20 hours ago! And neither are you. If your internal narrative is that you will always be the same and can't change, you won't see much progress. So, wherever you are right now, listen to me: We CAN change, we CAN evolve, and we CAN get better. If you are getting along in years, just know that even old dogs can learn new tricks! There are hundreds of ways I am different from the person I used to be. For instance, here's a story from my past that wouldn't happen to me today. Why? Because I make better choices now.

The blue lights came on in the rearview mirror. It was 2:15 a.m., the bars had just closed, and we were on our way back to Carrie's house for a late-night drink. There were three of us in the car, none sober, and I was driving. (Well, driving may be a stretch.) The officer ran up on our tail and turned his lights on, so I turned left down a side road that just happened to be where Carrie's house was located. I pulled slowly in front of her house and parked, then turned off the car with my hands on the steering wheel.

I stared straight ahead. Sucked in a deep breath.

"This is it," I said aloud, mostly to myself. "I'm going to jail."

What happened next stunned us all. After pulling in behind me for a brief pause, the officer sped away. Fast.

We let out a collective sigh of relief. From the back of the car, Steve said, "He must have gotten an emergency call more important than this."

At the time, I wasn't doing very well in life. I woke up the next day with another hangover. A glance at the clock showed that it was 1:30 in the afternoon. Should I get up and have lunch? Or close the curtains and sleep it off for another few hours? I called Carrie and said, "About last night," trying to ignore the headache that would last into the evening. And then I cracked another beer and made plans for later.

This cycle describes many nights and days in my young life. Back then, I was in my party phase. And that phase almost killed me.

Next came the work phase. It defined me and enveloped me, and I was the best of the best and worked harder than anyone else. I'm talking 60- and 70-hour workweeks and never knowing when (or even being able) to turn it off. That phase also almost killed me.

Then there was my false sense of balance phase. I thought I had it all figured out—I'd gotten the girl and the leadership job, but something was still missing.

Let's get one thing straight first. There came a time when things really started to change for me in a great way. And it all started with faith and forgiveness. Plain and simple. I gained knowledge and discovered that life is challenging, perfection is unattainable, and we must give ourselves and each other some room to operate without condemnation. The phases I just described were part of life. I was trying to figure it all out but stumbling sometimes along the way. Nowadays, I forgive myself for behaviors in the past that do not align with who I am. I ask for forgiveness from others when appropriate. I forgive others who have wronged me—or at least those *I have perceived* to have wronged me. It's amazing what different perspectives can do to opinions once they are shared in a meaningful way. It's even more amazing how much more enjoyable life is when you let go of the negative feelings you are holding inside. Let go of those judgments of others and those standards that no one can meet!

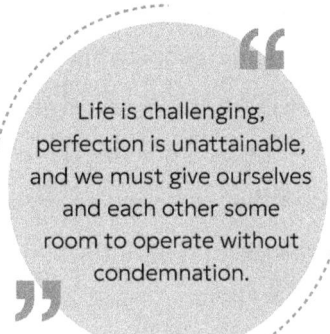

Life is challenging, perfection is unattainable, and we must give ourselves and each other some room to operate without condemnation.

Lack of forgiveness can cause major regrets. Life is full of surprises, and people are sometimes taken from us before we are ready. I have spoken with many people who wish they'd had one more conversation with someone—that they'd had to opportunity to mend a relationship, offer an apology, or forgive.

I was once asked to give a eulogy. It was the second eulogy I'd given for my wife's side of the family, so I must have done okay on the first one. The deceased was an interesting and flawed man (aren't we all?) and putting together the message was challenging.

I thought I had it down, though, and so we set off on the three-hour trek to South Florida, where I was to help the family in the healing process. On the way down, God spoke to me and put the lyrics of a song in my heart. The song was "Forgiveness[1]" by Matthew West. (If you haven't heard the song, I'd encourage you to give it a listen.) I just knew that God was speaking to me, letting me know that there were some people that were going to be in the room that needed these lyrics to help forgive the deceased and heal some wounds.

I pulled out my iPhone, found the lyrics, and chose a section that I find to be incredibly impactful and convicting. Next, I found the perfect place in the eulogy to insert these lyrics.

So here I was in a room of 100 or so, and finally I got to the lyrics. The room was somber, and I felt like we were honoring this man in an honest and respectful way. I told everyone that my heart was telling me to share these song lyrics. Then I took a deep breath and started. As I was right in the middle of delivering these lyrics, I got a little emotional and felt myself tearing up. Naturally, I expected the rest of the room to be on this emotional journey with me.

Instead, all at once, everyone burst out laughing. They were *loud*. As in *belly laughs* loud.

In all the public speaking I've ever done, this was by far the most confused I'd ever been. I caught myself, though, and powered through even though I was pretty embarrassed.

I finished up and went to sit next to my wife. I looked at her with one raised eyebrow, and she gave me a "not now, I'll tell you later" look.

Okay, are you ready for this? When we left the room, my wife pulled me aside and told me what had happened. Someone had forgotten to turn off the highlight reel of photos, which continued to play on the video screen behind me while I was speaking. At the exact moment I began to share the lyrics, a photo popped up on the screen that showed the deceased extending his middle finger to the entire room! He was apparently saying, "I got your 'Forgiveness' right here!"

So, there's the bonus takeaway for this chapter: Things aren't always as they seem! It's not always about me or you!

Life has been and always will be a journey filled with joys, sorrows, challenges, obstacles, wins, and losses. Accepting Jesus was a huge momentum-shifter during my journey of forgiveness. It took a whole lot of pressure off me and allowed me to realize that I was never going to live up to certain standards of living. In fact, no one could live up to the standard I was trying to live up to!

I do believe that Jesus died on the cross as the great sacrifice, and that He did so for all of us. This means we *all* have an opportunity to develop and maintain a relationship with God. What an incredible honor, and all we have to do is walk through the door. Forgiveness is a huge benefit of this amazing deal!

In 2011, Christ saved me, and in 2012, as an adult, I was baptized. At that point, things really started to change for me. This change didn't come for me through near-death experiences, near-miss DUIs, or hitting the bottom of the financial barrel (although those moments all played a part in leading me towards Jesus). It came from forging a relationship with Christ.

I also recognize that my path with Christ is still in progress. I am far from perfect, and the good news is that I am not striving for perfection anymore. I am striving for an ever-deepening relationship with Christ, a courage to share my faith with others, and the wisdom to lead my family toward the best possible decisions and outcomes.

Early on in my faith journey and struggles, a friend told me that God likes to give little signs along the way. This friend told me that God speaks to us using unique methods—and that we can hear Him, but we must give Him our faith.

One night, during a particularly rough stretch of insomnia (which I used to get quite often), I grabbed my Bible and spent half an hour journaling. Afterwards, I tried to remember the popular verse that everyone seems to quote. Where was that one "For God so loved the world" quote? I flipped through the pages and soon found the quote. John 3:16 says, "For God so loved the world that he gave his one and only Son, that whoever believes in him shall not perish but have eternal life."

Here came the sign. As I was walking back to the bedroom, I passed the house alarm system control pad. For some reason I froze and slowly looked to the left. And would you guess what time the display on the panel read? Yup. 3:16.

"What a coincidence!" Wrong. Be careful with having such a mindset. As life has progressed, I have learned that there are very few coincidences.

If that story didn't connect, here's another one.

Back in 2009, Tim Tebow was the quarterback for the Florida Gators. That year, they made it to the BCS National Championship Game, which was played on January 8, 2009. In that game, Tebow's eye black carried the inscription John 3:16, which caused millions of people to Google the meaning of it.

Exactly three years later, on January 8, 2012, Tebow played in his first NFL playoff game as quarterback for the Denver Broncos. In that game, against the Pittsburgh Steelers, he threw for exactly 316 yards. He averaged 31.6 yards per completion, which was a playoff record. Opposing quarterback Ben Roethlisberger threw an interception on 3rd and 16. And CBS's final quarter-hour overnight rankings? 31.6.

Coincidence? I think not.

ONE TO GROWN ON

Taking action to lighten the load:

1. If you are carrying extra baggage (be honest with yourself), consider giving or asking for forgiveness as a way to lighten the load and live a better life. Start with something small. Identify one situation and take the first step towards rectifying it.
2. Forgive yourself for past mistakes. You are not perfect! No one is. But you are valuable, so ask God for forgiveness.
3. Write down one or two things you have been ruminating on. What would you do differently next time? Write that down too.
4. Seek professional help if deep trauma within is preventing you from leading a strong life.
5. Be thankful—and show it! We are simply the stewards of what God provides in talents and treasures.

Faith and forgiveness can be quite hard. Doubts naturally creep in. Living up to Christian principles can be especially hard. Something my pastor Joby Martin says over and over again is, "Forgiven people forgive people." In other words, Christ paid the ultimate price so I would be forgiven of my sins, and therefore I am to forgive others just as God forgives me.

Still, it's not easy! Even in my own extended family, I have had a tough time forgiving. And on the flip side, I am certain there are people out there who I must ask for forgiveness, even if I don't yet realize it.

Simply put, forgiving is what we are called to do. Trust doesn't always come back into play, but still I forgive.

The point:

1. Withholding forgiveness can keep us from accomplishing big things. It can keep us from living a joyful, peaceful life.
2. No one is perfect. We must remember that there are very few people who are intentionally out to get us. Most people are doing the best they can based on what they think to be true.

Three more to explore:

The Bible
The Book of Forgiving by Desmond Tutu and Mpho Tutu
"Forgiveness" by Matthew West

Video Resources and Forgiveness Webinar

---

[1] Forgiveness by Matthew West, from the album Into the Light, released in 2012. Sparrow Records. Available on streaming platforms such as Spotify, Apple Music, and YouTube.

GET CLEAR ON YOUR MISSION/VISION/ PRINCIPLES (M.V.P.)

Establish good roots and enjoy the delicious fruits

I t is said that if you stand for nothing, you will fall for anything. So, what do you stand for? When you are faced with decisions in life, do you have a set of values by which to weigh the options?

What is your mission? What is your why, your purpose, and your reason to be? Author Stephen Covey once said, "Creating and integrating an empowering personal mission statement is one of the most important investments we can make." This requires some thought, and it can change over the course of a lifetime! People evolve, and there are different seasons, so don't worry about setting your mission in stone. Perhaps your goal is to be the best employee in your organization so you can provide for your family and have good benefits. Perhaps it's to create art through music, performance, or on a canvas to bring more joy to the world. Perhaps it's to build a business that empowers others to lead stronger and more fulfilling lives. Or maybe your goal is to change the face of politics and make the world a better place.

These are all just examples. This is where you get introspective and start thinking about your goals. If something popped into your head, write it down.

What is your vision for your life or business? How are you evolving and growing to live out your purpose? Where are you going? And more importantly, who is the person you need to become to better carry out your mission? For some of you, this means reconsidering your approach to your career, or perhaps your health and fitness. Travel is also important here to gain new perspectives. So are education and personal growth. Napoleon Hill had it right when he wrote, "Cherish your visions and your dreams, as they are the children of your soul; the blueprints of your ultimate achievements."

What are your principles? What guides you? What are non-negotiables in how you live your life? I'll give you some examples in a moment and walk you through an exercise. Franklin D. Roosevelt, the 32nd President of the United States, said, "Rules are not necessarily sacred—principles are."

My early days were jumbled with bad decisions and reactive behavior. Life happened to me—fast. I didn't take much responsibility for getting out there and making a positive impact on the world. There were many fun moments, but many of those moments were self-destructive and lacked deeper meaning.

Where are you today in your journey? The good news is that you do not have to wait as long as I did to begin your transformation. You can start today. And it can be immensely fun!

It is a process, though. Maybe you will accomplish most of the activities in the book, feel the difference internally, and notice a positive impact on your relationships and quality of life. On the other hand, you may put this book down when you are finished and do nothing for a while. You will only act when you are ready for the message. But just know that this book will allow you to plant seeds. Hang on to the lessons you learn and give it another read when you are ready—or maybe give it to someone else and ask them to read it. Then the two of you can discuss what you've learned and help one another work towards making change.

That is my goal for you. Stop with the actions that lead to bad mistakes and start with the actions that lead to good mistakes and growth. As leadership authority and best-selling author John Maxwell says, "Growth is a decision we make, not something that comes to us automatically." (Full disclosure: I am part of the John Maxwell Team and have been greatly influenced by his work over the years.) To experience tremendous growth, you must first get introspective and consider your principles. Doing so will help you build a strong foundation, stay connected to what matters most, and help you evaluate decisions that lead to a strong alignment in your values and how you are living.

Oxford Languages defines principles as "rules or beliefs governing one's personal behavior" and "morally correct behavior and attitudes." Earlier in my life, I valued parties, alcohol, cigarettes, and socializing with my friends. Now, some good did come out of this period. I still have some great friendships to this day. And sure, I had principles back then. But they were being boxed out by the instant gratification I was experiencing in my social life. And so, my career suffered. And my health suffered. My debts increased. I even skipped family events, which I now regret.

I needed clarity on my M.V.P.

In terms of identifying your mission, there is luckily quite a bit of research and guidance on the topic already. For instance, best-selling author Simon Sinek offers an array of formats to help via a TED Talk, a book titled *Start With Why*[1], and a corresponding workbook called *Find Your Why*[2]. One exercise that he mentions can serve as a good launching point for you. It is simply to complete the sentence, "To _____ so that _____." For my business, it's, "To <u>help clients and my online community</u> maximize opportunities and clear hurdles so that <u>they can live their best lives</u>." In my personal life, it's, "To <u>be the best husband and father</u> so that <u>my wife and kids have a great environment in which they can flourish</u>." I recommend reading all of Simon's works, but this exercise is a good jumping-off point for now.

Vision offers you a glimpse into the future you are trying to build. If my mission is X, and I am living in alignment with X, then where am I trying to take my life? How do I see it developing? Who do I see myself becoming to better accomplish these dreams? For some, a vision board is a fun and productive way to keep the vision at the forefront of your mind. If you search online for "vision boards," you will get thousands of examples. Here are a few suggestions:

1. Do one for the year, but also one for your long-term, bigger goals.
2. Include motivational phrases that have meaning for you.
3. If you include things like dream houses, cars, and boats, then make it stretch. But don't make it too "pie in the sky" relative to what you are doing on the annual board.
4. Include photos of family and friends in instances where you want to nurture and deepen relationships.

ONE TO GROWN ON

And now we will dig a little deeper into the P of M.V.P., because a good foundation of principles will help you deliver on your mission and your vision. How? By helping provide clarity.

Principles are very personal. If you haven't taken time to think about and write down your own principles, I suggest you do so. Here are a few ideas that should help you get started.

An exercise to discover your principles:

1. Consider some of the things you say yes to, and what you say no to.
2. Look at your calendar from the past six months and see how you fill your time.
3. Identify areas where you have been particularly emotional, negative, or positive.
4. Start writing down the underlying beliefs that drive your emotions and calendar.
5. Analyze the themes that emerge. Those are your principles.
6. Write down a draft of your principles and live with it for a month.
7. Take each one and write a paragraph that details why it's important. Write down examples.
8. Revise it as often as you'd like. You'll know when you have it "right."

Don't let anyone tell you your principles are wrong, or that you have too many of them. Your principles are exactly that—*your* principles. The issue, in some cases, is that we haven't taken the time to think through and identify them. The powerful part of this exercise is once you identify your principles and keep them at the forefront of your mind, you have a great filter to consider future decisions.

For my family, here is what we came up with. As you will see for us, faith is a big part of it. Perhaps some of these examples will help start the process for you:

> Don't let anyone tell you your principles are wrong, or that you have too many of them. Your principles are exactly that—your principles.

- We reflect God's light and strive to deepen our relationship with Christ.
- We love each other and show it.
- We are a team.
- We are honest with ourselves and with others.
- We take action. We are doers. We get it done.
- We are connectors, confident, courageous, calm, curious, caring, and celebratory of others.
- We can learn something from everyone.
- We pray.
- We laugh with each other and enjoy making people smile.
- We learn from mistakes and grow in wisdom.
- We are good stewards of our abundance.
- We intentionally add value to others each day.

I don't mean for you to copy these and try to adopt them. You must find your own principles—the ones that sing to you and bring joy to your heart.

ONE TO GROWN ON

I will make one suggestion, however, now that you've given my M.V.P. guidelines some thought. I'm sure you noticed there is a principle in my family's list that says, "We are honest with ourselves and with others." Well, I would recommend a version of that principle for everyone. Life is better when you are surrounded by people you have formed trusted relationships with. This applies in family life, with your friends, in business—everywhere. Trust is a major contributor to a fulfilling life.

Since trust is so valuable, we will focus on it here in more detail. As you develop your list of principles, you can spend some time thinking them through in similar fashion. Take each principle and write a paragraph about why you think it is important. Write down an example of its impact on your life, too.

Throughout my real estate career, part of my role has been to train and coach new agents. One question I always ask the group is, "What is the most important word in real estate?" (This is a question that elicits a broad range of answers.) "Sold!" someone would proclaim. "People!" another would shout. "Relationships!" "Listings!" And on and on it would go. Every once in a while, I'd get the right answer: "Trust!" And yes, that is the right answer. Because in both sales and life, we really don't have much if we don't have trust.

Afterwards, I break the word down and help people understand that trust is more than just character. "You see, your best friend, uncle, and even brother might not use you to buy or sell real estate when you are new. They may know you have the utmost in character, but they may not believe you have the right skills yet to handle their biggest asset."

I was first introduced to the components of trust by Stephen M.R. Covey in his book *The Speed of Trust*[3]. There, he breaks down trust into character and competence. I would go over some character traits with the team, and we would talk about honesty, integrity, loyalty, and giving back to the community. Then we would discuss competence, the need to become an expert on the market, learning how to properly market property, attending sales meetings and studying the contracts, and communicating this knowledge effectively. It looks like this:

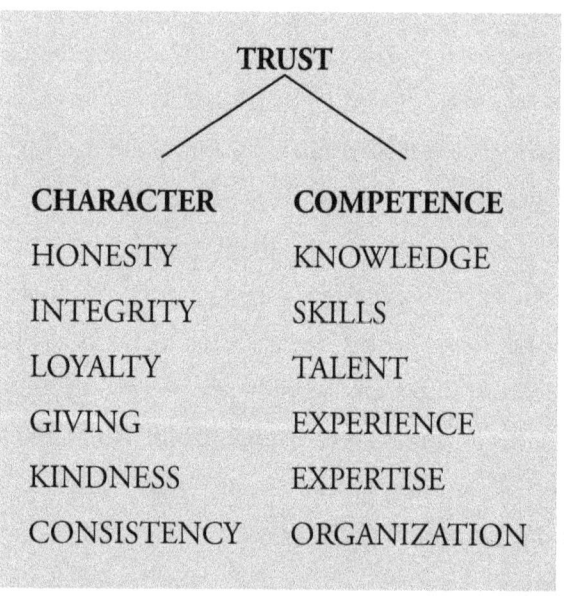

This approach applies to both our careers and personal lives. Through your principles expressed, you will display your character. To really succeed, though, you must develop and communicate great credibility. Become one of the best in your field. This can take time, but it is totally worth it.

Consider a major decision you must make when trust is strong versus when it is weak. Sticking with our real estate theme, imagine yourself sitting down with a real estate professional with whom you have a personal relationship. This person also has great moral character and has strong experience and results in the industry. You are considering buying your next dream home, and they come up with three or four options for you. One of the homes is a perfect fit. What do you do? Make an offer, likely.

Now, imagine the same scenario, only in this case the real estate agent is still experienced and has results, but their moral compass is questionable. You get the sense they only care about the transaction. They come up with the same three homes and *also* find the perfect fit. What do you do? Probably, you do more research, look at more homes, and fear you might end up missing something. Maybe you look at 50 homes when you should have bought one of the first few, all because you don't *trust* this real estate agent.

One day, I was previewing homes for sale with Gavin, an agent who worked for me. He was struggling with a client who had listed his home with us. The market was soft, the year was 2009, and buyers were in control because there was an oversupply of available homes. Gavin needed a price reduction on one of his listings. "I don't get it," he said. "The seller knows me. We flew combat missions together in the war. He knows I would tell him the truth on what he needs to do."

Timing was perfect. I had just read the Covey book, so I asked Gavin a few questions.

"Tell me more about your friendship," I said.

Gavin was right—they had a relationship built on trust under circumstances where the stakes were immensely higher than a real estate transaction.

"How many real estate transactions have you completed together?" I asked. I already knew the answer to this.

"Zero."

"Gavin," I said, "this seller knows you have the character trait of trust. What they don't know is whether you have the competence to handle a transaction with their greatest asset."

I asked Gavin if he had provided a thorough update and done a comparative market analysis (CMA) with facts and figures to support the price reduction request. He had not.

"Do that," I said. "Also, you have had quite a few real estate successes over the past couple years. Print out a list of all the homes you have sold—not to brag, but to isolate a few stories you can tell your client about sellers who made good decisions regarding price and how it paid off."

Within two days, Gavin had his price reduction. One piece of the trust picture does not equal results. The same is true of the inverse. And if you have all the competence in the world but you are a shady character? Well, that's even worse.

As Covey says, "Nothing is as fast as the speed of trust."

In other words, without trust, everything takes longer. Opportunities are missed.

And the tough thing about trust is this: It takes months (or years) to build it up, but just a few seconds to tear it down. Not fair? Well, fairness is a myth that we are told about in elementary school. In fact, I would argue that "fairness" is dangerously similar to entitlement, which can be a big problem. Trust is to be earned every single day, and it requires doing the right things even when no one is looking.

Let's look at how important trust is in organizations. After all, a great many of us own, lead, or work for a company. In a study that appeared in the Harvard Business Review (HBR) called "The Neuroscience of Trust[4]," Paul J. Zak writes:

ONE TO GROWN ON

"Compared with people at low-trust companies, people at high-trust companies report: 74% less stress, 106% more energy at work, 50% higher productivity, 13% fewer sick days, 76% more engagement, 29% more satisfaction with their lives, and 40% less burnout."

Clearly, trust is an important value and an abundance of it will make life much more worthwhile and less stressful.

So, what do you value? What are your principles? I encourage you to pause here and think about your answers if you haven't already. Write some things down. Maybe even create an artistic visual that you can see every day to remind you of your principles as you face the whirlwind. We have one hanging on our wall in our dining room.

The point:

1. Gaining clarity of your M.V.P. will help you develop a stronger foundation and succeed both personally and professionally. The stronger the roots, the more abundant and delicious the fruits.
2. Good principles are the foundation of good decision making and positive influence.
3. Principles are expressed in your character.

Three more to explore:

Start With Why and *Find Your Why* by Simon Sinek
The Speed of Trust by Stephen M.R. Covey
Change Your World by John Maxwell

Read Our Blog on M.V.P.

---

[1] Simon Sinek, Start with Why: How Great Leaders Inspire Everyone to Take Action, Portfolio, 2009.
[2] Simon Sinek, Find Your Why: A Practical Guide for Discovering Purpose for You and Your Team, Portfolio, 2017.
[3] Stephen M.R. Covey, The Speed of Trust: The One Thing That Changes Everything, Free Press, 2006.
[4] Paul J. Zak, "The Neuroscience of Trust", Harvard Business Review, January-February 2017.

FAMILY MATTERS

Make the time to relate with your relatives

What is your family like? What was your childhood like? What is your current family situation, and how do you fit into it? These are some questions to ponder and think through. Families come in all sorts of different cultures, shapes, and sizes, and many aspects of our family were chosen for us. How we approach family is a big part of our life!

Looking back, I realize I made a big mistake in my college and early professional years. You are going to hear me mention some mistakes along the way, and how necessary it is to make them. Make them, learn from them, and grow. I also will discuss the fact that there are good mistakes and bad mistakes. This mistake I am sharing now is a bad mistake—one of my few regrets. I got really caught up in my social life and neglected some important family moments along the way. I've always valued my family and appreciated them. In many ways, I had great relationships with almost all of my family. BUT I believe I could have made some better decisions along the way. For instance, I could've tried harder to attend a family member's wedding instead of that fun spring break trip, or made an extra visit to the hospital to see an aunt who was sick. I could've made one more phone call to a grandparent to ask them to tell me more about their life and our family history. Family is important. Family is history. And family is generally dysfunctional on some level and filled with love, conflict, and even drama. In other words, family is a jolt of real life!

My sister and I are very different. At times, I think she makes very poor decisions. But she is still my sister and I love her. And, we all make poor decisions from time to time.

My grandparents have all passed along now. I could have spent more time with them, found out more about their lives, and showed them more respect. I could have visited more and given them more of my time and attention as a young adult.

I've had two aunts, two cousins, a stepfather, and a stepmother pass away. I had great relationships with almost all of them, but I also feel I missed a few too many family get togethers over the years. In addition, I could have done better visiting while they were sick.

These are mistakes that, quite frankly, I do regret. But I can't change them. The only learning and future application will come in the form of other relationships going forward.

You see, family matters. And yes, so do friendships. But I realize now that I overdid it with friends and underdid it with family. And I get it—sometimes we have toxic or abusive relationships. If they cannot be mended through counseling, then you must make the decision to continue trying to build a connection or move on. Every one of us is valuable. We are humans and flawed, and we are searching for meaning and a way to add value to this world.

Sometimes family relationships need to end. Sometimes they need care and attention. Often, communication can solve estrangement. And sometimes with family there are complex scenarios in which you must decide between enabling or helping someone.

What is the difference, you ask? Here's a story that might help with the distinction.

We had to make a series of difficult decisions once with an older second cousin. We certainly love him a great deal, as he is a great guy who's taught me a lot over the years. I also think he sets a good example in some areas for our kids. At the time, he was living in Ocala with his mom and considering the next chapter in his life. I convinced him to move to Jacksonville and live with us for a bit while he got himself set up in a new job and on his feet financially.

What I did not know, however, was that he had a serious problem with money management and supporting himself financially. When times were good and the insurance business was booming, he was okay. But he was definitely on the "make it and spend it" program, too. And like me earlier in life, he was also good at spending more than he earned.

Well, he was supposed to live with us for a few months and then get his own place. But all did not go as planned. What happened was, he bounced around with work—first for some local companies, then with a business he started on his own. But he was never fully engaged in what he was doing. He also spent every single dime he earned (and then some) on trivial things and never saved anything (I have first-hand experience with this problem, which I will share with you later). All in all, he was with us for a year, during which time he put heavy strain on our financial situation, not to mention my relationship with my wife, Jessica. At first, some of the decisions I had to make came off as looking insensitive. I was caught in a pickle between fending for my nuclear family and being accused of not supporting family. It was a no-win situation. And even though I think we navigated it as delicately as possible, it still caused a few big fights.

Over time, Jessica came to see that what we were doing was in fact enabling this cousin and not helping him. He was 100% capable of earning a living, he just wasn't getting out and doing it. Their relationship started to strain, and finally he made the right call to move back in with his mom before his relationship with us worsened.

These days, he is making a decent living for himself. I have no idea if he is saving for retirement, but it's his call if he wants to work his entire life.

If we had continued down that same path, we would have been enabling him to continue to make poor decisions both financially and otherwise. Oh, and by the way, he agrees with everything I'm saying! Some of us have deep-rooted issues with money that date back to our childhood. If we were taught as kids that money is the root of all evil, or that those with money are snobs, or that money doesn't grow on trees, then we adopted that mindset. Think about it. We then take an approach in life to get rid of money as soon as we get any, make excuses about it, or hide it and not be generous. Or we act like there isn't enough to go around and think, "I can't get enough of it, so I'll just rely on someone else or the government to provide it." All of these mindsets are financially irresponsible.

There are ways we can be there and support our extended family members, and many of these ways do not need to involve finances. For instance:

We can provide emotional support to someone going through a rough time.

We can provide inspirational support to someone who needs a boost.

We can provide physical support to someone who needs a helping hand.

We can provide mentoring and wisdom to someone struggling with a decision.

The key is to identify whether you are helping someone or enabling them. What's the difference? Helping someone leads to them improving and getting better with our help and guidance, whereas enabling is when we hold some sort of power over them and satisfy our own need for control.

> Helping someone leads to them improving and getting better with our help and guidance, whereas enabling is when we hold some sort of power over them and satisfy our own need for control.

Enabling causes someone to continue to rely on us, whereas helping allows them to flourish and improve on their own. It's like that adage about giving a person a fish versus teaching them how to fish.

It's family though, and if it was between our home or the street, I guarantee that cousin would be living with us. Family gets special treatment. And sometimes, it is next to impossible to not border on enabling!

I would also recommend you slow down a bit and be present when you are with family. When I'm with family, I sometimes catch myself thinking about tomorrow, or the next big presentation, or a speaking opportunity. That's not good. There is so much power in being present and not getting caught up in tomorrow's stressors or today's distractions.

Once I was taking a walk with Elliott, who at the time was three years old. Now, I am also a runner, so when I am walking or running, my primary goal is usually exercise. I like to keep moving. But on this particular day, Elliott stopped a few times abruptly to smell a flower. After the third flower, I was getting a tad frustrated.

"Let's go, buddy, keep on moving," I told him.

He'd keep up with me a bit—those little legs of his churning along—and then he'd stop again, pull a flower to his nose, and take a deep breath in. He seemed so content just standing there with the flower. Looking at it, smelling it. Suddenly I thought: *Wow.* To be content with that. Also, I'd started thinking on some level that he was trying to draw out the experience and make it last longer—this walk with his daddy. I realized that I was also content watching him do this. It made me think of my grandfather, who always made it a point to "stop and smell the roses."

So, I let go of my agenda, and do you know what we did? We smelled just about every single flower from that point on, all the way back to our house. A run/walk that normally would have taken 15 minutes took 45—and I loved every single one of those minutes!

Jessica and I have also started putting our devices in our bedroom during the evenings when we are all together. This allows for an emergency check every so often, but disallows the constant distraction of the device. It also ensures that we are all actually paying attention to one another. In a 2018 study, Visit Anaheim[1] interviewed 2,000 families and found that the average quality time spent per weekday was 37 minutes. While that number jumped to two hours and forty minutes on the weekend, the sad part is this: According to TechJury, "Americans spend an average screen time of 5.4 hours on their mobile phones daily." Maybe we can adjust the ratio a bit so we can better connect with the people that mean the most to us.

ONE TO GROWN ON

To better connect with family:

1. Call (not email, not message, not text) someone in your family you haven't spoken with in a while to reconnect.
2. Add a weekly check-in with an extended family member either face to face or voice to voice. It doesn't need to be the same person every week.
3. If you have family that lives nearby, schedule some time together once per month to have lunch or coffee. Face-to-face interaction always provides more of a connection.
4. Think in advance about the questions you will ask during these interactions. Do you know about their childhood? About your family's history? About how they view the world?
5. For those who are married, get serious about consistent date nights with your spouse. Do it. Start with what you can manage. If you have young kids, once per week can be tough, so aim for once a month at a minimum.
6. Turn off your devices at dinner time, bedtime, and any other key times where it is important to let your family know you are present.

For those who have had rough family upbringings and traumatic experiences along the way, I feel for you. I wish we could rewrite history and change some of the hurting that people have experienced. But history cannot be rewritten, and so I would encourage anyone who needs professional help to seek it out to release themselves of the past. Life is a beautiful, fragile thing, and the thought that the past somehow inhibits people from living out their dreams and their best lives really gets me fired up! We are here, right here and now, and we all can make decisions to get help, live life, improve, forgive, and grow loving and trusting relationships. And yes, you need to be intentional with this. Because approaching life in an intentional way is how we will create and attract great things.

In fact, the word of the year for me is "intentional." I plan on being intentional with our most valuable resource: time. I will carve out time for what matters most, and for me that means my family and faith. When I am with family, I am really with them. (Well, most of the time. But we are all works in progress, aren't we?!) This is an area of constant development for me, and that's why I'm being intentional. I want our son and daughter to grow up valuing family and our time together. I want them to see what it means to be truly *present* with people. And when I am at work, I am intentional there, too. I am focused. I do not let life's distractions carry me away from my job (unless there is some sort of emergency). This level of focus allows me to then feel no guilt at the end of the day when I disengage and spend quality time with my favorite people!

Let's learn from poet and thought leader Maya Angelou, who said, "I sustain myself with the love of family."

The point:

1. The most important relationships in your life are the ones you have with family. Some require effort and patience. In the end, it is all worth it.
2. If you are in a toxic or abusive relationship within your family, create new and strong relationships outside of that dynamic to rely on instead.

ONE TO GROWN ON

3. Help others! Help your family! Identify the line between helping and enabling. Is the person you are helping getting better and acquiring skills to be self-sufficient?

Three more to explore:

Tuesdays With Morrie by Mitch Albom
The Four Agreements by Don Miguel Ruiz
"Family Life Today" by FamilyLife Podcast Network

Resources For Further Research

---

[1] Visit Anaheim, "Study Reveals American Families Spend the Most Quality Time Together While on Vacation," 2018. https://www.visitanaheim.org/articles/post/visit-anaheim-study-reveals-american-families-spend-the-most-quality-time-together-while-on-vacation.

FLOCK WITH THE RIGHT CREW

Who you spend time with matters. A lot.

Look around you. Who do you spend the most time with? You don't get to choose your family—that dysfunctional beauty chooses us. You do, however, get to choose your friends, your life partner, your work colleagues, and your mentors. So choose wisely!

This is not a chapter about judging others (although it might at times come across that way). Who we spend our time with shapes us and is a reflection of us. If money is important to you, it is said that your net worth is the average of the five people you spend the most time with.

I'm not sure about that math, frankly. What I am sure about is that spending time with people who possess good values and positive mindsets absolutely is better than surrounding yourself with negativity and complainers.

Have you ever been in a room and had someone just walk in and brighten the place up? Their positive energy and character changed everything, right? Conversely, have you ever been in a room when someone walks in and the energy drops? It's like they turned on a vacuum that sucked all the positivity out. Here's a tip: Don't be that person if you want to lead a fulfilling life. Don't surround yourself with people like that, either. If you aren't sure what sort of person you are, ask around. And be open to constructive feedback if you want to improve.

The key is to become the person who exhibits the behaviors that you look for in your crew. After all, birds of a feather flock together. If you are a positive person with a growth mindset, you will likely attract that and repel the negative. But if you surround yourself with negativity and poor values, it will take a toll. You may also need to conduct an honest self-assessment to identify why you are attracting negativity.

> If you are a positive person with a growth mindset, you will likely attract that and repel the negative. But if you surround yourself with negativity and poor values, it will take a toll. You may also need to conduct an honest self-assessment to identify why you are attracting negativity.

If you were part of a strong peer group with good values growing up, you have a bit of a head start. If not, you have a chance to do something about your current scenario. Now, I have heard some people say you need to drop friends to move up in life. And maybe that's true. But I would pump the brakes on that advice a bit before you jettison anyone from your squad.

For sure, there are certainly some people we need to move on from. For instance, if you have friends who are physically or mentally abusive or keep putting you in bad situations. Sometimes, though, you might just need to sit them down and have an honest conversation. "Here is where I see us right now. Our friendship is important to me, so I'd like things to change. I'd like us to work on X, Y, and

Z," you can say. Whatever the issue is, give people a chance to learn and grow with you. You may end up helping someone who really needed a lift.

Perhaps this book or another one recommended within these pages would be a nice gift. Start a book club with your peers. See who is willing to join you on your journey. For those who make the decision to stick to their old life-draining ways, well, you have a decision to make as to how much time you want to invest in them. Remember, time is our most precious and valuable gift. We only have so much of it, and we can never know exactly how much!

I have two important pointers for you now. First, notice that I am talking about values and mindset. I would encourage you to not surround yourself only with people who share the same or similar backgrounds and ideas about life. There has been such a shift recently where people get so incredibly angry at others who possess different ideologies, religions, or political affiliations. What happened to having conversations? To open and friendly debate? People now have this idea that they cannot be friends with those who hold different values and beliefs. To me, that is ridiculous. We need to learn how to come back together with diverse ideas and engage one another respectfully in the process. In *Long Walk to Freedom*[1], Nelson Mandela said, "No one is born hating another person because of the color of his skin, or his background, or his religion. People must learn to hate, and if they can learn to hate, they can be taught to love, for love comes more naturally to the human heart than its opposite."

When people come together from diverse backgrounds and with ideas, the greatest progress is made. Character traits such as integrity and willingness to do the right thing should be the measuring stick when it comes to developing friendships and considering and evaluating ideas. Where someone comes from or what they believe in should *not* be the measuring stick.

Second, I am in no way suggesting we ignore people in need. There are people out there who have been dealt a serious blow in life, and they need us to acknowledge them and help them in whatever ways we can. This stretches beyond just the financial, too. We can help others develop a growth mindset.

There are amazing people around me. I have a solid crew. We don't spend as much time together as we did in our early 20s (think of the 90s/2000s TV show *Friends*—that's how much we were together) as we are "grown" with families now. But when we do get together, our time is filled with love and laughter. I have their backs and they have mine, and that's a good feeling.

Friendships like these are critical.

My first job was with Merrill Lynch Credit Corporation as a client services representative. I answered the phones and took mortgage applications. The awesome thing about that place was that I developed some lifelong friendships. But at the same time, I was really a screw-up. I called in sick from hangovers more than the average bear. I dated other employees. I found ways to game the system. I was a really poor employee. There was a flash of being good when I received a temp assignment to go out and serve as a credit specialist for someone on maternity leave. That was more challenging and enjoyable. (So, a quick side lesson here on that note: Make sure what you do is challenging and enjoyable.) When I returned from that assignment, though, there was a hiring and promotion freeze. So, I was unable to move into one of those roles full time. I left the credit division and joined the financial advisory team. I was still answering phones, still bored, still not challenged. Eventually, I got myself laid off.

ONE TO GROWN ON

A couple months later, I found myself in Miami for a friend's bachelor party. We had invited one of my friends who lived there to play golf with us. I'd helped him get a job at Merrill a couple years earlier, and they had relocated his position to Miami. He was preparing to leave that role, and so he asked me, "Would you be interested in interviewing for the spot?"

The idea of getting hired into what would have been a promotion from the job I had just been laid off from was an intriguing challenge. Also, I was living in Jacksonville at the time and, from a career standpoint, the prospects were bleak. So I took a flier and went down to interview a couple weeks later.

This story brings us to the next critical relationships to foster: those with mentors. I am fortunate that I have a mother and father who each, in their own way, instilled good values in me and served as early mentors. My mother is the most caring and empathic person I know. My father is a brilliant businessman and got me started early reading books of all kinds. We don't get to choose our family, though, so I'm going to spend more time in this chapter focusing on areas where you can make good choices. And for me, even though the foundation was there, I still screwed some things up out of the gate when I left college. So, when I showed up in Miami for this new job, I clearly needed some guidance.

Enter David McWilliams into my life.

David made an instant impression on me during our very first interview, when he decided to give me a shot. He was a larger-than-life, values-based leader who commanded (not demanded) the respect of everyone on his team. The position I was hired into was basically a business analysis and reporting function. Over time, I built it into much more, but the true benefit of this role had little to do with the function.

The real value in that role was not even the compensation. In fact, living in Miami on that wage led me further into debt. The *real* value was in the example David set, which helped me envision where I wanted to go in life. He was a true leader.

Every Monday morning, I was fortunate to be part of his "inner circle" staff meeting. I was given the opportunity to contribute during those meetings, which taught me a lot about how communication drives effectiveness. Also, my desk was outside his office, and because he usually left the door open, I would hear him having conversations and learn how he communicated with his people. I got to travel to some of the conferences he led and work on the visuals for his speeches. This experience was so incredibly valuable. You truly could not attach a dollar amount to it.

I watched as he navigated conflict and disarmed anyone who got heated with him. I saw that he put family and faith commitments on his calendar first and the important business meetings next.

This was all helping to shape me—but only because I was ready for it.

David was also the first person to put a John Maxwell book in my hands. That started me on a lifelong learning journey that introduced me to many author/mentors whom I have never met.

David passed away in 2021. I hope he felt appreciated for the powerful and positive impact he had on me and many others. I've let him know over the years through calls and thank-you notes about each promotion I've received. For you, I am hopeful there is a David McWilliams out there. Because mentorship is special and life-changing when done right.

ONE TO GROWN ON

Be open to mentors pouring into you. Finding good mentors is one of the most important decisions you make in life. Choose wisely.

And ask yourself: Are these relationships **relational** or transactional? Do your mentors genuinely care about helping in your development, or is there some sort of ulterior benefit they are focused on?

Are they **growing** personally and professionally or are they stagnant? Do they practice what they preach with a commitment to lifelong learning?

Are they **values-based** or do they rationalize poor decisions? Are they living out good values on their success journey or do they just want to win at all costs?

Are they **honest** or patronizing? Do they give you real feedback to help you improve? Or are they just going through the motions and afraid to hurt your feelings with honesty?

Mentors are vital. So, you must have a mindset of always being coachable and willing to learn. I learn from people every day—it's a benefit of keeping company smarter than me.

Another former boss of mine is Christy Budnick. She's an example of a powerful, balanced leader who always brought both empathy and strength to the table. She once explained to me a tough call she'd had to make regarding giving someone critical feedback. She took the time to walk me through the entire call, which she had clearly handled so skillfully. As usual, I felt I got a little bit smarter after listening to her, and so I thanked her for sharing her wisdom.

Another part of your flock—the most important part—is your life partner. For me, that's Jessica, my amazing wife. She is strong, tough, beautiful, intelligent, caring, and a great mom. In short, she makes me better. We have our challenges and struggles now and then, but we take them head on and grow together.

All these qualities shone through over a period when we were having issues getting pregnant, and then with miscarriages when we *were* able to conceive. Only those who want children and have gone through these trials know the emotions involved—the stress, the sadness, the fear, and the self-doubt. It was a tough time, and Jessica was a superstar along the way. Elliott and Raelynn are here with us today as a result of her determination and resolve. I am so proud of her, and we have such little blessings in our kiddos. We were given less than a 5% chance of success at one point, but thankfully we kept on—although in many ways it wasn't much of a hassle if you consider the action involved! The real issue was getting our hopes up and then having those hopes crushed month after month. That part was not easy.

Finding a loving partner is one of the most important decisions you make in life. Choose wisely, and ask yourself:

Do they respect you for who you are? Or do they try to make you into something you aren't?

Do they battle against you or battle challenges with you?

Do they lift you up or tear you down?

Do they listen to you or talk over you?

Surround yourself with supportive people. Doing so will build your confidence and assist you in knowing your self-worth. Constructive feedback is good, yes, but your crew should primarily be encouraging, supportive, uplifting, and empathic. There is enough negativity out there in the world—we don't need our inner circle bringing us down.

On this topic, have you seen the Adam Sandler movie *Happy Gilmore*[2]? If not, you've got to watch it! When I think about allowing good inputs to come in and minimizing the negative junk that comes into our brains, I think of Kevin Nealon's cameo performance as Gary Potter, in which he discusses the flow of energy.

Below is that exchange.

Gary Potter: "Oh yeah. Lotta pressure. You gotta rise above it. You gotta harness in the good energy, block out the bad. Harness. Energy. Block. Bad. Feel the flow, Happy. Feel it. It's circular. It's like a carousel. You pay the quarter, you get on the horse, it goes up and down, and AROUND. It's circular. Circle, with the music, the flow. All good things."

Happy Gilmore: "Yeah, alright. Good to meet you."

Happy Gilmore: [to himself] "Psycho."

Well, he may come across as a psycho in the movie, but there is certainly a major benefit in what he was saying. Surrounding yourself with good people and positive influences throughout life's journey is one of the smartest moves you can make.

To grow and deepen relationships and allow the best inputs, you must:

1. Assess your friendships. Pour more time and energy into the relationships that have greater purpose.
2. Join a group of people with similar interests. Try making a new friend.
3. Find a podcast to listen to that is positive and uplifting. One great example is "School of Greatness" by Lewis Howes.
4. Pay attention to what inputs you allow to enter your brain. News is almost always negative and divisive. Find the right balance—one that allows you to know what is going on

but that doesn't depress you and ruin your life. This is not hyperbole!

5. Find a cause that interests you, then join a group and volunteer. You will make a difference and meet some cool people along the way.
6. To acknowledge and carry on the legacies of influential people in your life who have passed away, make a list that includes their names and one or two important things each person taught you.

Remember how I mentioned that I was first given a John Maxwell book by David McWilliams? That was back in 2002. In 2021, I was able to introduce Dr. Maxwell to our real estate company as the keynote speaker for our annual kickoff meeting. I also eventually completed a course and attended a virtual event to become a certified John Maxwell Team member. These are two life list items for me, and they very much have to do with what mentors and books helped welcome into my life.

The point:

1. Good, diverse people enrich our lives and help us through tough times.
2. The inputs we allow ourselves are crucial. Good books and podcasts can be like mentors.
3. Finding a good life partner will enrich your life. It will make the days warmer, your spirit lighter, and growing old more enjoyable.

ONE TO GROWN ON

Three more to explore:

Think and Grow Rich by Napolean Hill
Extreme Ownership by Jocko Willink and Leif Babin
Team of Rivals by Doris Kearns Goodwin

**OTGO Community Preview Flock
With the Right Crew Webinar**

---

[1] Nelson Mandela, *Long Walk to Freedom*: The Autobiography of Nelson Mandela, Little, Brown and Company, 1994.
[2] *Happy Gilmore*, directed by Dennis Dugan, performances by Adam Sandler, Julie Bowen, and Christopher McDonald, Universal Pictures, 1996.

JOY IN SIMPLE THINGS

Look up from the screens

Technology is amazing. But you know what's more amazing? The human minds that are creative enough to *innovate* these new technologies.

The issue is that certain technologies have shifted our focus toward looking for joy and true entertainment in our electronic devices rather than with each other. You know how much joy and satisfaction can also come from the very basic and *simple* things we innovate? And a lot of these experiences don't require a lot of money!

Let me explain. In college, my friends and I would sometimes get tired of the studying, partying, eating, and drinking that accompanies campus life. But instead of allowing ourselves to get bored, we would create new ways to entertain ourselves. We could make a game out of anything. One fun game we played was called "sideline drill." We would throw a football back and forth, leading the receiver towards an imaginary boundary line. The receiver would have to make the "miracle" grab while keeping two feet in bounds, often diving and falling out of bounds in the process. We could do this for hours on end. Seriously. Running back and forth, catching a ball, and often falling down in the process—it was FUN!

This next example was and is dumb, and I don't recommend it. But it still illustrates the point beautifully. You know those playpens filled with little plastic balls that they used to have in McDonald's and Burger King? Yes, as 20-something-year-olds, we would occasionally dive into those pits. But that's not even the best part. Once, a couple of those little plastic balls made it back to the dorm with us. One night after grilling some burgers, I threw one of those little plastic balls into the air and tried to stab it with a grill fork. I was unsuccessful, and so the little plastic ball simply bounced off the fork and landed on the ground. Then a buddy picked it up and threw it to me again, and again I unsuccessfully tried to stab it. Next, I handed him the fork and I tossed the ball his way and *he* tried to stab it. Just like that, a game was born. For the next week, after classes and before parties started, we would stand outside in front of the dorm (to the amusement of many passers-by) and toss this little ball to each other while the other attempted to stab it out of the air with a grill fork. (The passers-by gave us a wide berth.)

It was an obsession, and we could have easily deemed it to be impossible after a few hundred—possibly thousand—attempts. But sure enough, after my arm was getting sore from this unusual motion, I tried a risky uppercut maneuver and pierced that ball with the grill fork. I don't know if I'd ever celebrated anything more intensely up until that point. A crowd gathered around me and watched as I celebrated like Tiger Woods used to after winning a major. (They say the definition of insanity is trying the same thing over and over again and expecting a different result. But the reality is that sometimes it works to be persistent.)

There are so many things you can do that require little or no major financial investment: hiking, biking, walking, running, exercising outdoors, reading, writing, playing guitar, surfing, paddle boarding, throwing a baseball/football around, playing basketball or soccer, swimming, gardening, drawing, painting, playing hacky sack, sitting around a fire pit, telling stories, skateboarding, stargazing, and even sex (at least I hope sex doesn't cost you anything). Have more things you can add to that list? Go for it! And yes, you may argue that a surfboard or a bike or a guitar costs money. And you're right. But once you own it, it costs very little to maintain, and you can use it hundreds of times after that initial purchase. (Also, used surfboards and bicycles are a good deal cheaper! Keep that in mind.)

Speaking of things that don't cost much money. One Christmas, we were running late for a family gathering. Being late has always driven my wife crazy. (She and I butt heads on the difference between being late for a work appointment versus a personal gathering, but I digress.) On the way, we remembered we were supposed to bring a dessert. A quick stop at the gas station (all that was open), and we were on our way with a $5.99 special Christmas cake with bright red and green frosting in a plastic pan. It was perhaps the ugliest looking sweet treat I have ever laid eyes on, so it was *perfect* for a Christmas party!

We proudly—or not so proudly, if I really think about it—positioned our contribution next to other far more beautiful homemade desserts, many of which were presented on platters alongside nice cake servers and utensils. As you may have guessed, our little cake went untouched. Jessica's dad saved the cake, and at our next gathering a few weeks later (at our condo) the cake showed up again. We all had a chuckle, and at the end of the night this little gem once again had been ignored and remained perfectly intact. We popped it in the fridge, thinking we'd eat it sometime before the expiration date.

Well, our next gathering was around Easter. The cake was showing signs of wear, and it was smeared all over. No way was anyone going to eat it, but guess what? We still put it on display for all to see. By this point, it was amusing for everyone.

This back and forth went on for a while, and we started trying to outdo one another. Once the cake was wrapped as a Christmas present and opened, once it was prearranged to be delivered to me on my birthday at a restaurant, and once it was even hidden inside another cake and discovered while cutting into the other cake. If a bird hadn't picked up the cheap cake and taken it with him after we left it outside one day, my next plan included a drone for delivery. How cool would that have been?

Simple. Silly. Thoughtful. Joyful.

If you keep your eyes open and let yourself remain a kid at heart, you will find that life is filled with all sorts of fun and games. Sitting at the breakfast bar at my mom and stepfather's home, I once took off my wedding ring and gave it a spin on the granite counter. After some initial eye rolls and irritation from the wife, she gave it a spin. Twenty minutes later, my stepfather and I were in a major competition trying to see who could spin it and have it remain spinning for the longest duration of time. I have the record to this date, with a spin that lasted one minute and twenty-eight seconds. This simple activity gave us serious enjoyment—and for years we have had rematches.

Another part of the joy equation is having an outward focus on others. You will derive great pleasure from doing kind things for others! And it doesn't matter whether they even *know* what you're doing for them. These so-called random acts of kindness will lift both your spirit and that of others. They have a great multiplier effect. Imagine

ONE TO GROWN ON

thousands more people committing one or two acts of kindness each day. Imagine those acts then brighten someone's life, and in turn that person starts committing their own random acts of kindness. We could see a major ripple effect throughout the world. One little act of kindness can have a major impact, believe me. I have been on the giving and receiving end.

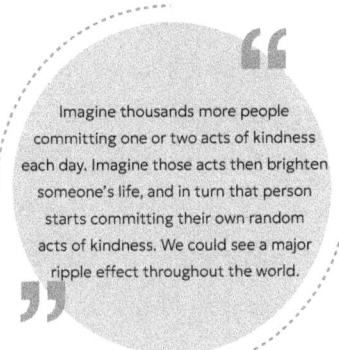

When I was 12 years old, I went to a parade in downtown Stuart, Florida. There I was, enjoying the bands and the music along the way. But then I noticed there was one local school that had no uniforms for the band, and the band's instruments didn't have the same level of sparkle as the other school bands. This prompted me to ask some questions of the adults around me at the time. Some schools have less money than others and cannot provide the same resources, they told me. Well, I decided I wanted to do something to give back to the community. My wishes manifested differently than I imagined, though, and we landed on serving a mission that was shocking to us at the time.

A friend and I had started researching local organizations in need of support, and we came across a home for abused children called Hibiscus House. We really didn't know how to process the concept of abused children, but we knew we wanted to help them in any way we could. I couldn't imagine what these kids were going through. They'd had to leave their homes and move because of abuse from a parent, and they'd had to deal with feelings of being unloved. Hibiscus House was in the middle of a capital campaign meant to raise money for a new facility. With this new facility, they could take in more children.

Anyway, we recruited some more kids and founded Children Helping Other Children (CHOC) in the late '80s. (Disclaimer, I notice there is an organization of the same name in South Florida today. There is no relation between our group and that one.) We did odd jobs around the neighborhood for donations, and all the proceeds went to Hibiscus House. We raised somewhere around $1,000 over two summers, so our impact wasn't large financially. But we did raise awareness for Hibiscus House via some local media outlets that covered our story.

I love seeing this sort of attitude nowadays in young people. I know I have drifted away from this level of compassion over the years, so I have been correcting that recently with my time and my treasure. As a family, we are becoming better stewards of our blessings every day.

How about you? Is there a cause or an event you can jump into? It can be really simple and seemingly small. Consider the following example of a relatively small yet life-saving impact. This touching story illustrates how the little things can make a big difference—even if it doesn't seem like it.

The following is adapted from "The Star Thrower[1]," an original story by Loren Eiseley:

One day a man was walking along the beach when he noticed a boy picking something up and gently throwing it into the ocean.

Approaching the boy, the man asked, "What are you doing?"

The youth replied, "Throwing starfish back into the ocean. The surf is up and the tide is going out. If I don't throw them back, they'll die."

ONE TO GROWN ON

"Son," the man said, "don't you realize there are miles and miles of beach and hundreds of starfish? You can't make a difference!"

After listening politely, the boy bent down, picked up another starfish, and threw it back into the surf. Then, smiling at the man, he said, "I made a difference for that one."

This story affects me every time I hear it.

The "Random Acts of Kindness" movement is nothing new. It is important to note the exponential value that both the giver and receiver of kindness gain. A 2020 study written by Erika Stoerkel for positivepsychology.com[2] shares 14 benefits of acts of kindness[1]. Let's look at a summary of her conclusions:

Giving and receiving kindness can increase:

1. Oxytocin
2. Heart health
3. Self-esteem/self-worth
4. Optimism
5. Strength
6. Energy
7. Serotonin
8. Healing and calming feelings
9. Well-being
10. Good fortune

Giving and receiving kindness can reduce:

1. Blood pressure
2. Stress
3. Social anxiety

4. Aches and pains
5. Depression

When you are looking to increase low-cost and low-tech joy, do the following:

1. Think of a unique game that involves some out-of-the-box thinking. (Caution: I would avoid any game with a grill fork or other sharp object. In hindsight, that was pretty stupid of us.)
2. If you want to start a conversation and really learn about people at a posh party with beautiful food presentations, buy a cheap cake in a plastic container. Arrive at this posh party, put the cake out, and observe everybody's reactions. I know this advice is oddly specific, but just try to have some fun with it. Basically, what I'm saying here is to do something that might be a bit contrarian in nature. Something fun and lighthearted that will grab attention. Get creative!
3. Execute an act of kindness. Do one *today*. And one tomorrow … and the next day!

When I was growing up, there was this wicker monkey figurine at my Grammy and Grandpa's house. One day, my Grandpa decided he would hide it from me, and then I would go look for it. Once I found it, I would hide it from him. On and on this went for years. Now, as an adult, my wife and I do the same thing with various stuffed animals around the house. We hide them in little spots for each other and for our son and daughter to find. When you unpack a bag on vacation, open the medicine cabinet, or peel back the covers at night and find that little stuffed animal, it always brings about a smile and reminds someone that they are loved. Do me a favor and steal this little game of ours. Trust me, it won't disappoint.

We all experience negativity, sorrow, anger, loneliness, and other feelings we would often rather avoid. The goal here is not to ignore or sweep those feelings under the rug—that isn't possible, nor is it healthy. The point is to understand that we have a choice to make. We can either wallow in the negative or adopt strategies that help us move towards the positive.

The author Rudyard Kipling once said, "Teach us delight in simple things, and mirth that has no bitter springs."

I had to look up the word "mirth." According to Dictionary.com, it means "gaiety or jollity, especially when accompanied by laughter."

The point:

1. Bank on the fact that there is so, so much joy to be had in simple and playful ways with others. And this joy can be experienced in far greater depth than the type we experience with screens. You can find truer enjoyment in *places* and *activities*.
2. You can find lots of enjoyment and strengthen bonds when you seek to do good for others—and it costs virtually nothing. You just have to look for the opportunities to embrace your inner child.
3. Kindness towards others often benefits you as much as them. Sometimes it even benefits you more!

Three more to explore:

The Happiness Advantage by Shawn Achor (Watch the TED Talk too. It's hilarious and impactful.)
10% Happier by Dan Harris
Chicken Soup for the Soul by Jack Canfield

Read Our Blog on Joy In Little Things

---

[1] Loren Eiseley, *The Star Thrower*, Harcourt, 1978.
[2] PositivePsychology.com, "Random Acts of Kindness: A Guide to Spreading Joy," https://positivepsychology.com/random-acts-kindness/.

FEAR IS THE BIGGEST LIAR

Step forward into growth or backward into comfort

I have done the public speaking thing hundreds of times. But I wasn't always comfortable or confident. In school, I managed to mostly avoid the task of public speaking. I made excuses, or I figured out a way to produce a video, or I teamed up with others and picked up slack elsewhere. This is not advisable, though, and in hindsight the practice would have been excellent.

During my professional career, it hasn't been easy to avoid public speaking. Once I had to give a 30-minute talk about one of the new initiatives we were rolling out at an offsite retreat and how the people in the room would be impacted. Even though I knew my stuff, the anxiety I felt in the weeks before came in great waves. I'd be fine one night and then unable to sleep for hours other nights. I simply couldn't control my rampant thoughts.

Finally, after weeks of agonizing, I stood at the podium and looked out at the audience: a blend of executives and high-ranking salespeople. I was very nervous leading up to this moment, but relaxed into it and enjoyed it once I got going. My bigger issue was the splitting headache due to drinking too many cocktails the night prior—a feeble attempt to squash the jitters that came along with public speaking. It hadn't worked, and I'd neglected to set my alarm. Only by the grace of God had I managed to wake up on time.

I had spent hours preparing, and I was ready. But the worry still came.

If only I knew then what I know now. In breaking this down, I am hopeful that I may help you take on any fear, whether it's public speaking or something else. CNBC.com shares an article by Benjamin Snyder entitled "The 10 Biggest Fears Holding You Back From Success[1]." Here are those ten fears:

1. The fear of inadequacy
2. The fear of uncertainty
3. The fear of failure
4. The fear of rejection
5. The fear of missing out (FOMO)
6. The fear of change
7. The fear of losing control
8. The fear of being judged
9. The fear of something bad happening
10. The fear of getting hurt

Let's try out an exercise. In this exercise, we will ask ourselves a few questions about fear. These are universal questions and should be asked to address any fear, but we will use public speaking (a common fear) as our example.

Why was I afraid? In thinking about it, I realized my view was quite self-centered. I was worried about what others would think about my performance and my delivery. I worried about what my boss would think—if it would stall my career or help me get a promotion. My thinking was all, "me, me, me." That is a problem! The more we focus on ourselves, the more we think we are the center of the universe and the more stress we put on ourselves to deliver. If we place that much pressure on ourselves, we are all but destined to fail.

Who was I afraid of? You know what's funny? Even if we have a self-centered view and have trouble shaking that view, the people in your audience don't see things that way! One thing is for sure: They will attach far less weight to your moments in the spotlight. By the way, I've learned over time that it is possible, and advisable, to care deeply for others—but that you don't always have to care what they think about you.

What was I afraid of? Stuttering? Forgetting my talking points? Tripping on stage? Even if one of these things did happen (and most of the time they don't), no one in the audience would care. And by the way, if someone snickers because you mess up on stage, that says more about *them* than it does about *you*. Oh, and you're the one courageously on stage, not them!

What's the worst that could happen? And is it a likely outcome? A healthy level of fear is okay. After all, it keeps us from doing really stupid things! (For instance, once, as a kid, I tried to jump off a roof using a large kite, which I thought would allow me to fly. That was not smart! And it was painful. Fear would've come in handy back then!) But with good, calculated risks, I have developed over time a powerful mindset. I now know that the most challenging and difficult scenarios are what shape us. So, when it comes to public speaking, I came to realize that if the worst ever happened, I would learn from the moment and use it to improve. I promise—taking good risks is a big part of living life to the fullest!

One thing I know for sure is that worry is a wasted emotion. The best we can do is face the fears we have and take necessary steps to combat them. Every minute spent worrying carries with it an opportunity cost. You could be feeding your mind with positive reinforcement instead.

> "One thing I know for sure is that worry is a wasted emotion. The best we can do is face the fears we have and take necessary steps to combat them. Every minute spent worrying carries with it an opportunity cost."

Think back, briefly, on your time spent worrying. How often did the worst come to fruition? Probably never, right? Or at least very rarely. If your answer is often, then it may be time to assess your perspective on life.

Here are some suggestions to tackle your fears:

1. Focus on others, how you can make them feel, and the value you're adding to their lives. This applies to both public speaking and social anxiety. In the case of public speaking, if you can give them something they can use or make them feel better about their day, you will succeed. Even if you trip and fall and stutter the whole time!
2. Keep things in perspective. If you attribute too much hype to something, maybe consider how small it is in the grand scheme of life. Ask yourself if that thing will matter one year from now, or even one month from now.

3. Whatever the fear is, face it. Take baby steps to overcome it. If you are afraid of flying, try taking a short commercial flight before signing up for pilot lessons.
4. If you can, gamify the steps you must take to tackle your fear. Have a contest with a friend or colleague. Do whatever you can to make it (as) fun (as possible).

Your mindset plays a big role. How do you view yourself? How do you view your failures? How do you approach life? For years, I've helped people in sales become more proactive in their approach. Reactive means you are on someone else's agenda. Proactive means you are intentionally moving the needle in your favor.

Another way to look at it: Was something intentional or an accident? Do you influence what happens in your life? Or does life happen to you? In her book *Mindset: The New Psychology of Success*[2], Dr. Carol Dweck defines a growth mindset and a fixed mindset. She says, "In the fixed mindset, everything is about the outcome. If you fail—or if you're not the best—it's all been wasted. The growth mindset allows people to value what they're doing regardless of the outcome. They're tackling problems, charting new courses, working on important issues. Maybe they haven't found the cure for cancer, but the search was deeply meaningful." Imagine what adopting a growth mindset could do for you. Imagine how much it would help you face your fears!

Mindset and Life Approach Options

Proactive: You act and cause things to happen.
Intentional: You cause specific things to happen that you focus on and prioritize.
Growth: You believe that the experience is valuable even if the outcome isn't planned.
OR
Reactive: You wait for things to happen.
Accident: You then act *after the fact*.
Fixed: If it doesn't work out well, the experience was wasted. Negativity ensues.

If you spend too much time worrying, you cannot give your best. And guess what? You cannot make up for it tomorrow. Admiral William H. McRaven said, "I sometimes fell short of being the best, but I never fell short of giving it my best." If you adopt that mindset, fear will begin to subside in certain areas. And you will gain confidence.

Facing fear requires courage. If you don't consider yourself a courageous person, there is most likely a root cause. You were told when you were young that you wouldn't amount to anything. You were chastised for making mistakes. You had fearful parents. You had teachers that encouraged you to stay in your lane and not take risks. These root causes are at the heart of your internal programming. And the key is to rewrite the program!

There is a chapter in this book called Powerful Programming, in which we address how to combat fears and weaknesses with positive self-talk. Without question, taking courageous action and experiencing the associated reward is an amazing way to reduce fears. Again, the key is to take action. To improve and experience greater results, we cannot rely on the same plan that got us where we are today.

Over time, I learned how restricting it is to stay inside of your comfort zone. To grow, you must become comfortable OUTSIDE of your comfort zone. That is where lessons are really learned and progress is made. If you are comfortable every day, you probably aren't growing much.

Another common fear is that of commitment. This fear can manifest in many ways, and it often has its roots in our upbringing. But while it is true that our childhood can influence our behaviors throughout lives, it is also true that we can work on ourselves and improve. Having divorced parents is one of the root causes of commitment issues. And because a full 50% (or more) of marriages end in divorce, quite a few children must overcome this trauma in later relationships.

My parents got a divorce when I was ten years old and my sister was five. It took a long, long time to overcome my commitment issues. But in the end, addressing the issue and healing has been much better than living a lonely life.

In my early years, my commitment issues went way beyond just my relationships. Heck, I found it difficult to commit two hours to go to the theater and watch a movie. Getting me to commit to attending a social function in advance was harder than catching a cat who preferred social isolation.

But over time, I grew. And now, as you know, I have developed and live by a set of principles. These principles help me determine where and to what I should commit time and energy. And then I stick with those commitments as best I can.

During the early part of my leadership journey, I also had a fear of not knowing. In other words, I was scared that I didn't have all the answers. In some cases, I probably even gave some bad advice as a result. This fear also limited my ability to connect to anything deeper than surface-level stuff. Sure, I would enjoy my team and have a great time with them, but we rarely connected on a deep, intimate level. All because I feared failing to impress them! What an ego I had! In trying to have all the answers and be the best leader, I wasn't allowing myself to be vulnerable and authentic with people. My way of leading was a façade.

Those walls have come down over the years. I have now shared many intimate moments with my staff. For instance, I shared the upcoming arrival of our first child at a sales meeting and burst into tears doing it! I've told them about some of the troublesome moments I had as a young adult during coaching sessions. In some cases, I may even *overshare* with someone who asks a simple question. They get a personal story to paint the picture instead of a simple response! "That was probably more than you wanted," I often tell these people when I'm done speaking.

What is your biggest fear? Flying? Roller coasters? Spiders? Public speaking? Being vulnerable? Death? The dentist?

Shift your focus. Start living with purpose and authenticity. Be yourself. Don't be so concerned with others' perception of you. Discuss your fears with someone who cares about you or someone who shares (or shared) the same fear. Take steps to learn more about what it is that frightens you. You'll discover so, so much about yourself.

Fear of rejection is also quite common. Take the case of Jill, for example. Jill was a strong real estate agent who experienced great success. She would win more often than not, but she would also occasionally discount her fee even though she knew her value was in line with her full rate. While working with her, we uncovered an underlying fear of rejection. Due to this fear, she often did whatever it took to win the business—even if it meant operating at a minimal dollar-per-hour basis. We addressed her fear with her, and she came to understand her value as a human had nothing to do with whether or not she earned a piece of business. Then we helped her understand that it was as much about her deciding to work with the prospects as it was them deciding to work with her. With a new and empowered mindset, she went on to thrive at a whole new level. She started feeling more confident in charging a fee that was in line with her value. Prospective clients could now tell her no, and she would be able to realize that it simply wasn't a good fit. She knew rejections did not reflect her worth.

In coaching hundreds of salespeople and leaders over the years, I discovered that some people also have a fear of hearing "yes." Fear of hearing "no" is obvious—many people fear rejection, as it can bruise the ego and diminish our self-worth. But fear of yes took me a minute to identify and help correct in those I was coaching. I realized that, for some, success was a foreign concept that could be viewed with condemnation. These individuals grew up in households that were lacking, and they heard their parents make negative comments about "rich people" or state that "money is the root of all evil." (The proper phrase in 1 Timothy 6:10 is, "For the *love of money* is the root of all evil …") Others felt they were not worthy of success or simply didn't deserve it. A moment in their past had caused them to think less of themselves.

Another issue in hearing yes is that some folks lack preparedness. This can be an issue for new salespeople—what if their prospect actually says yes and agrees to meet with them? Are they prepared? Will they fail? Will they know the answers to the client's questions?

One solution for this challenge is to develop a package (digital or hard copy) of information about your product or service that you can rely on in meetings. This is a crutch at first, but it eventually becomes a supporting piece as you develop the necessary skills. The sales process is something that serves every single one of us—even those of us who are not in sales. We will devote an entire chapter to it later.

What about dating? Are you holding back from asking someone out because you fear the actual date? Instead of focusing on that, focus on the other person! If you ask them good questions and genuinely care about their answers, everything else will fall into place. And honestly, what's the worst that could happen? If you get turned down, will that matter three months from now?

What will you do today to face your fears?

I have struggled with various fears throughout my life. But most of them never came to fruition. My fears seemed to develop over time, as I was fearless as a youngster. Today, my biggest fear is that I will have lived a life without significance. Writing this book is part of me *facing* that fear. It is a very big step toward living life to the fullest and allowing myself to be vulnerable at times.

Looking back, some of my most memorable moments have come during my time speaking on a stage. Up there, I can make a great impact. And I've even shared the stage with people I admire greatly! Thankfully I conquered my fear of public speaking and made it through. The nerves are still there, but I'm much better at dealing with them and getting through my delivery. It helps that I care a great deal about what I am doing.

ONE TO GROWN ON

The point:

1. You are uniquely and wonderfully made, but you are not the center of the universe. You aren't even the center of your own "universe." Take that pressure off yourself.
2. Most **F**EAR is **F**alse **E**vidence **A**ppearing **R**eal.
3. Worry is a wasted emotion.

Three more to explore:

You Are a Badass by Jen Sincero
The Power of Intention by Dr. Wayne W. Dwyer
Mindset by Dr. Carol Dweck

Read Our Blog Fear Is The Biggest Liar

---

[1] Ruth Umoh, "The 10 Biggest Fears Holding You Back From Success," CNBC, May 18, 2017. https://www.cnbc.com/2017/05/18/the-10-biggest-fears-holding-you-back-from-success.html.
[2] Carol S. Dweck, Mindset: *The New Psychology of Success*, Ballantine Books, 2006.

HABITS AND RESULTS

WINNING THE DAY

The importance of the "Morning Kickstart"

Developing good habits will change your life. Replacing bad habits with good ones changed mine. The little things, when done repetitively over time, will have an amazing impact thanks to the power of compounding. This is true in finances, relationships, health and fitness, parenting, and pretty much every other area of life. The concept of planting seeds and cultivating them over time is not a new one, although it can be very difficult to carry out. I owe much of my success to the many volumes written on the power of habits, especially that of the morning routine. John Maxwell said, "All is well that begins well." If I can positively influence the way you begin your day, you'll have gained at least one incredibly valuable lesson from this book.

Now, routines can sound a little boring, and they do have a tendency to turn into ruts. So to put a truly positive spin on things, I'd like you to start referring to your morning routine as your "Morning Kickstart." That sounds more fun and energetic already, doesn't it?

I believe the results of the Morning Kickstart that I lay out in this chapter will make you want to take this part of the book seriously. We are literally talking about life and death stuff here. For instance, here are the results I've gained from implementing my Morning Kickstart:

- My morning affirmations helped me quit smoking.
- My morning exercise helped me lose 30 pounds.
- My morning gratitudes help me look for the positive in all situations.
- My morning meditation and prayer reduced my blood pressure.
- My morning review of my life list helps me achieve my goals.
- My morning reading greatly reduces the presence of negative emotions and poor reactions in my life.
- My morning note-writing allows me to share my appreciation with others and makes them feel good.

Amazing, huh? My advice would be to start with one new thing (i.e., writing, praying, or exercising) this week, and then add one more thing each week until you have a full Morning Kickstart that suits your life. Oh, and try to start today! Even if it isn't the morning right now, start right now and then work the routine into your morning tomorrow!

If you're telling yourself, "I don't have time for this, I have too many things going on in the morning, I have to get the kids ready in the morning, I am not a morning person, blah blah blah," stop! Self-limiting beliefs are a thing of your

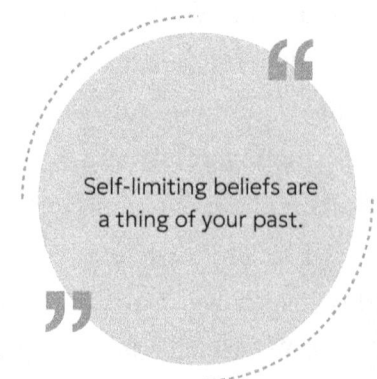

Self-limiting beliefs are a thing of your past.

past. There are people out there who can barely walk because of serious autoimmune deficiencies, and yet they *still* have Morning Kickstarts! I know people with multiple businesses and six kids, and they still make time to start the day off right. Cut the excuses. The possibilities in your life will prove to be endless when you stop limiting yourself. DO IT NOW! Yes, I am yelling. Talk to me in a month and let me know if you are better or worse off for it. If your work includes overnight shifts, use your best judgment to decide when you should schedule your Morning Kickstart.

There are two fundamental ways to approach life: as either a player or a victim. Players know they have decisions to make and how to respond to external stimuli. Victims believe that everything happens to them and that they have little or no control over what happens or how they respond.

Now, let's discuss some of my morning rituals, starting with gratitudes. Being grateful for what you have plays a huge role in attracting new and better things into your life. This one is easy for many. But for others, it's not. If you are down to your last dollar and staring at massive credit card debt, if you are recently divorced and looking at moving back in with your parents because you cannot make ends meet, or if you just received an awful diagnosis, this is a difficult exercise. But it is critical.

Being grateful helps you look for the positive in life even when your circumstances seem grim. It is good for our health. It is good for our relationships. It helps us maintain positive energy, which is crucial.

I incorporate my gratitudes into prayer, as the two go hand in hand. I am so thankful for what God has blessed my family with. After reading a passage from the Bible, expressing my gratitudes is the second thing I do each morning. Sometimes it is very powerful to share your gratitudes with your loved ones. They will start sharing back, and next thing you know, you will both be starting your days with great energy.

In addition to your ongoing gratitudes, look for three new things every 24 hours to be thankful for. Doing so will train your brain to look for the positive in all circumstances. There is a great deal of good out there, but we need to know how to look for it.

You may decide to find someone to be your gratitude accountability partner and then share your three new gratitudes with them every day. Some people actually post their gratitudes on social media. Another alternative is to begin a gratitude journal and write down what you are grateful for every day. No matter how you do it, the important part is to do it every single day. It is a game changer.

Here is a list of some of the benefits derived from daily gratitude practice. The points on this list come from various studies conducted over the past two decades:

1. Gratitude can help people cope with stress and build stronger relationships[1] (Ilene Rosenstein, psychologist and associate vice provost for campus well-being and education at USC).
2. Gratitude improves physical health[2] (2012 study published in *Personality and Individual Differences*).
3. Gratitude can improve mental health, reducing negative emotions like envy and frustration[3] (Dr. Robert Emmons, UC Berkeley).
4. Gratitude improves sleep[4] (2011 study published in *Applied Psychology: Health and Well-Being*).

5. Gratitude triggers dopamine and serotonin, enhancing performance, motivation, willpower, and happiness (*The Power of Thanks*[5], by Eric Mosley and Derek Irvine).

Need I continue?

After gratitudes comes silence, prayer, or meditation. For me, gratitude is a big part of my prayers. After I pray, I sit in silence for eight minutes, completely still, and focus on my breathing. There is science behind this practice that says our brains are not wired for all of the external stimuli and distractions that are thrown at us (or that we seek out) each day. Taking eight minutes in the morning to just breathe allows us to better prepare for the day and even minimize our reactive nature to distractions. It also helps reduce anxiety. It does take some practice, though. Getting to a point where you can quiet your mind for even two minutes is a challenge. And that's what I would suggest: starting with two minutes. I did. Then I worked up to six, and now I'm at eight. Some meditate for 30 minutes or longer. That's not me right now, but maybe it will be one day.

And when your brain starts to wander from breathing, don't fret! Just let the thoughts come and go while you breathe. For those who remember *The Karate Kid* from the '80s, just think of what Mr. Miyagi says to Daniel LaRusso: "Breathe in, breathe out. Breathe in, breathe out." This can help you prepare your mind for the day ahead.

There are different ways to meditate and many, many books written about meditation. You can also find hundreds of podcasts dedicated to guided meditation. For instance, I sit in a comfortable chair and breathe in through my nose and out through my mouth. I rest my arms on the arms of the chair with my palms facing up and my thumb and index finger barely pressed together. I don't know why I do this—but it is comfortable, and I've seen yoga people do it. I set an eight-minute timer on my iPhone and then I sit there and focus on my breathing. If a thought comes to me, I let it come and go. I don't break my focus or try to analyze what to do—I just let it go. I always feel a little more amped up for the rest of my Kickstart and exercise after I get through this eight minutes. I'm not fully sure why, but it works for me.

In a *Forbes* article published in 2015 called "7 Ways Meditation Can Actually Change The Brain[6]," Alice G. Walton shares the impact of meditation backed by research at UCLA, Yale University, Johns Hopkins, and Harvard University. The results:

1. Meditation helps preserve the aging brain.
2. Meditation reduces activity in the brain's "Me Center" (also known as our wandering mind, which randomly goes from thought to thought).
3. Meditation's effects rival antidepressants for depression and anxiety.
4. Meditation may lead to volume changes in key areas of the brain.
5. Just a few days of training improves concentration and attention.
6. Meditation reduces anxiety and social anxiety.
7. Meditation can help with addiction.

Here's an incredible quote from that article as well:

"In 2011, Sara Lazar and her team at Harvard found that mindfulness meditation can actually change the structure of the brain. Eight weeks of mindfulness-based stress reduction (MBSR) was found to increase cortical thickness in the hippocampus, which governs learning and memory, and in certain areas of the brain that play roles in emotion regulation and self-referential processing. There were also decreases in brain cell volume in the amygdala, which is responsible for fear, anxiety, and stress—and these changes matched the participants' self-reports of their stress levels, indicating that meditation not only changes the brain, but it changes our subjective perception and feelings as well. In fact, a follow-up study by Lazar's team found that after meditation training, changes in brain areas linked to mood and arousal were also linked to improvements in how participants said they felt—i.e., their psychological well-being. So for anyone who says that activated blobs in the brain don't necessarily mean anything, our subjective experience—improved mood and well-being—does indeed seem to be shifted through meditation as well."

The next part of my Morning Kickstart is a positive reading. I've provided plenty of good reads for you in the end of each chapter in this book and in the list in the appendix at the end. This list can keep you busy for years. And there are new great books coming out every month. Don't bite off too much—we are simply talking about ten minutes of reading each morning.

This book was written in a small chapter format, so one idea is to go back through these chapters for five minutes each to read one at a time. In 20 days or so, you will have reinforced all the behaviors throughout. What we read can have a major impact on our development over time.

In addition to the mentors in my life that I've known personally—my parents, family, and those I've worked for and with—I count the authors of books that I've read and studied as mentors. They have helped me in so many ways. I am better at making decisions, remaining calm under fire, being patient when called for, acting when appropriate, listening more and talking less, and being more strategic with my time. Many of these things were taught to me by mentors, but I fully grasped them thanks to reading books.

Not a big reader? Let me present this idea. Pick up the biography of someone you admire. Grab a book by someone who is successful, someone who has had a positive impact in history, or any book by John Maxwell. If you do, you will open up a whole new world of learning and growing.

Next is affirmations, which we will go deeper on in the next chapter. Affirmations are positive assertions that confirm truths. If something isn't true for you now, you can program your brain to move you towards your desired future-state via affirmations. Do not skip this—there is way more power in positive self-talk than you can possibly comprehend (unless you have already) studied the science behind it. Affirmations help you tap into the power of your non-conscious brain and influence the habits and activities you choose to engage in. Without affirmations, you will remain on autopilot much of the time, completely unaware as to why you are unable to change your behavior. Your conscious brain is limited in its ability to influence your behavior, so utilize affirmations to tap into where the real power lies.

ONE TO GROWN ON

Ever make a New Year's resolution and then wonder why you've reverted to your "normal" behavior by February? It's because of your programming. Remember, if we want to change our behaviors, we must change the program.

Affirmations, to be effective, must be:

1. Written
2. Stated in the positive
3. Stated in present tense
4. Reinforced by feeling the emotion that is associated with the statement

Let's look at a few examples of effective versus ineffective affirmations.

Effective: I enjoy the rewards of earning $250,000 or more per year.

Why? Stated in current terms, specific and positive.

Ineffective: *I want to earn $250,000 per year.*

Why? Stated in future tense and as a yearning rather than a truth.

Effective: I make healthy decisions regarding what I put in my body to experience normal blood pressure and my ideal weight of ____.

Why? Stated in current terms, focused on action, has specific targets, and positive.

Ineffective: *I am not a smoker. I do not smoke.*

Why? Stated in the negative. The subconscious will focus on the word "smoker," and you may be worse off for it. In other words, steer clear of Bart Simpson detention-style affirmations!

These should be written 20 times each day for a period of 30 days to be effective. Think of them as your mental push-ups. As you write, allow yourself to feel the positive emotions associated with whatever you are affirming. Over time, that voice of self-doubt will begin to quiet down, and you will begin taking the right actions. At first, I focused on repeating one affirmation at a time in areas where I wanted to grow. Now I have a handful of affirmations that I write or state five days per week to reinforce the values and the behaviors I wish to live by.

Now we come to a review of the "Life List." Some call it a Bucket List. Whatever you call it, the point is that you need one! Simply having a list is a good start for success. This is different than your personal and professional goal setting exercises each year, which is also important. This is a list of things you want to accomplish and *become*. You may want to earn $250,000 this year, which could go on both your goal list and your life list, but you also may want to buy a new house or car, which might not be realistic this year. The house and car would go on the life list. My life list includes wanting to learn Spanish, playing guitar at expert level, being a scratch golfer, going skydiving (maybe), hiking the Appalachian Trail, and donating $1M to charity. These are all life list items that I can then break down into smaller tasks on my annual goals exercise. Each morning, take a moment to review this list and pick a couple items to visualize. As is the case with your annual goals list, the life list should be written down and accompanied by as many visuals as possible. You can ultimately create a vision board of your life list with photos that represent what success looks like to you. There are even some apps that help with this project. When you review the list and visuals each morning, close your eyes and imagine yourself on that special trip, in that home, behind the wheel of that car, or playing your brand new guitar. Whatever it is for you, get that image in your mind.

Next, let's focus on one of the best random acts of kindness today: note-writing. This part of the Morning Kickstart is where we begin to add value to others' lives and make them feel good. When we ask people how many emails they receive in a week, the answer is often hundreds to thousands. And when we ask how many text messages someone receives each week, the answer is often dozens to hundreds.

But when we ask people how many handwritten notes they received over the past week, the answer is often zero. Rarely, the answer is one or two. If you want to stand out from the crowd, send handwritten notes often. Don't overthink it. Use one to say thank you to someone, to congratulate someone, or to let them know that you were simply thinking about them. I have written thousands of handwritten notes over the years, and I can tell you that they have a very positive effect on people. And while the motive is to make people feel genuinely good, the returns via business opportunities and hearing about how much people appreciated the gesture makes it even more worth it.

Finally, once you speak with your doctor, develop an exercise regimen. Don't overdo it. Thirty minutes a day is plenty. Depending on your mobility and current health level, you may want to start small. The Japanese term "kaizen" applies here. Kaizen is continual, minimal, and measured improvement over time. If you don't exercise right now, then perhaps start by tracking your steps on your phone or watch. Aim for a 1% improvement every day for a month and see what happens. The next step might be to get a stationary bike or perhaps go jogging. You could work your way up to a marathon. If you are already a long-distance runner, perhaps dial the running back a little and add swimming or some resistance training, which is better for the joints. It's your call. The key is to get the blood flowing and the energy up in the morning as part of your daily Morning Kickstart.

If I were a begging person, this is where I would insert the beg. I want for you a fruitful life. But it is very difficult to gain that life and serve others if you are in poor health. The good news is that you can always move in the right direction and improve.

My Morning Kickstart has contributed to much of the progress in my life. Here is my current Kickstart broken down into time investment:

	My Current Kickstart
Gratitudes and prayer:	1 minute
Meditation:	8 minutes
Positive reading:	5 minutes
Write affirmations:	8 minutes
Review life list and visualize:	3 minutes
Two handwritten notes:	5 minutes
Exercise:	30 minutes (put on a positive podcast or uplifting music during)
Total kickstart:	**60 minutes**

To start your day in winning fashion:

1. Break everything down into manageable steps. If you currently do nothing, pick one step and start small. Decide to

engage for 30 days. Exercise would be primary. Gratitudes are also easy and take very little time.
2. Create your own Kickstart. Mine works for me, so you need to find what works for you. Build it up. Add in some more exercise as you go.
3. Don't fall into a rut. My Kickstart is flexible. For example, sometimes I lift weights, sometimes I run, and sometimes I swim for the exercise portion. Don't run the exact same path and distance every day—that can get boring. (There will be a whole chapter later that further discusses routines and avoiding ruts.)

Of course, you will need to develop other daily habits outside of these, and we will touch a bit more on habit development and cessation along the way. For now, starting the day with great habits can make a great difference in your life. It can help you set the foundation for better habits and actions throughout the day.

The point:

1. How you begin your day will have a major impact on your health and your personal and professional success. It will prepare you in many ways to be more proactive and also allow you to better respond to external stimuli.
2. Focus inward first. Then set out to add value to others. It's like the oxygen mask on an airplane concept—it's tough to assist others if you are busy gasping for air.

Three more to explore:

Miracle Morning by Hal Elrod
Ninja Selling by Larry Kendall
The Answer by John Assaraf

OTGO Community Preview Morning Kickstart Webinar

---

1. Science Blog Staff, "Practicing Gratitude Can Have Profound Health Benefits, USC Experts Say," ScienceBlog, November 13, 2020. https://scienceblog.com/512298/practicing-gratitude-can-have-profound-health-benefits-usc-experts-say/.
2. Amy Morin, "7 Scientifically Proven Benefits of Gratitude," Psychology Today, April 4, 2015. https://www.psychologytoday.com/us/blog/what-mentally-strong-people-dont-do/201504/7-scientifically-proven-benefits-of-gratitude.
3. Robert Emmons, "Why Gratitude is Good," Greater Good Magazine, November 16, 2010. https://greatergood.berkeley.edu/article/item/why_gratitude_is_good.
4. Linda Wasmer Andrews, "How Gratitude Helps You Sleep at Night," Psychology Today, November 21, 2011. https://www.psychologytoday.com/intl/blog/minding-the-body/201111/how-gratitude-helps-you-sleep-at-night.
5. Eric Mosley and Derek Irvine, *The Power of Thanks: How Social Recognition Empowers Employees and Creates a Best Place to Work*, McGraw-Hill, 2015.
6. Alice G. Walton, "7 Ways Meditation Can Actually Change the Brain," *Forbes*, February 9, 2015. https://www.forbes.com/sites/alicegwalton/2015/02/09/7-ways-meditation-can-actually-change-the-brain/.

POWERFUL PROGRAMMING

High C's to quench the mindset

We need to go deeper on programming. It's just that important. We have established that our non conscious (also referred to as subconscious) is far more powerful than our conscious brain and that it is the underlying cause for many of the actions we take. Our experiences, our relationships, our traumas, our successes, our environment, our joys and sorrows—all of these get recorded and lie beneath the surface of our consciousness. It's similar in concept to an iceberg, where the bulk of the matter is beneath the visible surface.

We can influence that massive part of our brain through proper programming. A large part of the Morning Kickstart from the last chapter is designed to help us with this programming. If you take all the steps of the Morning Kickstart together, you have a system that can influence your life in a positive way.

I used to think that affirmations were as silly as Stuart Smalley made them out to be on the earlier days of *Saturday Night Live*. But now I know the science behind the power of our non-conscious brain. There are endless resources that discuss the science behind our mindset—and a big part of our mindset is determined by our self-talk, self-image, and self-esteem.

I was leading a webinar once when someone asked, "Do affirmations really work?" The answer is either yes or no, it's up to you. If you are just repeating something over and over again with no emotional or visual connection, the answer is no. You are merely fooling yourself. However, if you believe you can make changes in your life and reach a place of confidence, then affirmations can absolutely have an incredible, powerful influence on your outcomes.

As mentioned in the last chapter, my Morning Kickstart helped me quit smoking. I had quite a few false starts before succeeding. When I first wanted to quit smoking, I would employ my willpower. I would try to convince myself it was the right thing to do. I would set New Year's resolutions. I would try and try, then relapse, and then just be a "social" smoker. Then I would only smoke when I drank, so I started drinking more. It was a vicious and unhealthy cycle in which I was having the same problem that thousands of early-January gym-goers have every year. New Year's resolutions usually don't work when only using the conscious part of the brain. Life is much harder when you try to employ *just* willpower and not direct programming. To be effective, we must put our non-conscious brain to work.

How do we do this? There are a few ways. Our non-conscious brain is like a recording device that doesn't judge. Part of our behavior is impacted and caused by our experiences and results over time. The inputs we allow into our minds are also responsible for our behavior. Is it the bad news on TV every night? Silly YouTube videos of dogs and cats? How about the people in our lives we listen to? Are they helping us grow or tearing us down? And finally, what are we telling ourselves?

The non-conscious brain believes what it is told via repetition. In other words, we can program this part of our brain to influence our behavior and help attract good things into our lives. This is not motivational BS—it's science.

In the *Yale Review of Undergraduate Research in Psychology*[1], Michelle M. Lee, Kate M. Turetsky, and Julie Spicer of Columbia University analyzed dozens of studies on the effects of affirmations. They found that[2]:

1. Affirmations can improve effectiveness and overall well-being. This occurs through the reduction of worry and stress, which leaves us with more time, energy, and effort to accomplish productive tasks.
2. Affirmations can lead to improved memory function.
3. Affirmations can improve abilities to focus and increase our discipline to stay focused.
4. Affirmations reduce the reactive biases we have when we receive information that is contrary to our beliefs.
5. Affirmations can improve our feelings of self-worth.
6. Affirmations can reduce stress and increase our ability to cope with negativity.

Now, this programming part of our mindset is only part of the battle. Simply wishing for things and visualizing them won't make them materialize. The result is that our actions will start to align with our mindset, and then we will make better decisions that move us towards the things we want or need and away from those we don't need.

When coupled with a solid Morning Kickstart, good affirmations will engage your reticular activating system (RAS) in a great way. Your reticular activating system is the part of your brain that will seek out what you program—whether good or bad. When you buy a new car and think you are being unique, and you then see it everywhere, that is your RAS at work. You have researched the car, looked at pictures of it, and you keep programming it into your brain. Now it's all around you! Trust me, those cars were there before. Your RAS just filtered it out. I recently did some landscape work in our yard, and now I notice a certain type of palm tree all over the place. They were there before, but I am only aware of them now. (By the way, if you're ruminating on fears and anxiety, your RAS will focus on those too. That's why this chapter and the prior one are so incredibly important.)

> Our actions will start to align with our mindset, and then we will make better decisions that move us towards the things we want or need and away from those we don't need.

All this RAS talk reminds me of a story. I was playing golf once with my uncle in Maryland, and we were on the 12th hole. I hit an amazing drive that left me about 100 yards from the center of the green. There were no threats (water, preserve, out of bounds) between the hole and me, but there was a sand trap on the other side of the green that was well off to the right. I focused on the proper spot, the center of the green, and started my backswing. When the club was in motion, here was my inner dialogue:

"I have a pretty good score going."

ONE TO GROWN ON

"It's amazing through 12 holes that you haven't hit a ball in the sand."

"Why would you say that?"

"Don't think about the sand."

"I hope I don't hit it in the sand."

"The sand isn't close to being in play."

You can guess what happened next. I hit the ball in a manner that sent it directly into the sand—meaning I hit it "thin" so it would travel farther than my selected club should travel, and I "sliced" it hard so it peeled off to the right. It's amazing the power our thoughts have and how they impact our actions. Focus on what you want, and your RAS will deliver. Focus on what you don't want? Your RAS will try to deliver that too.

I will share an example now of one of my favorite affirmations: the High C's. To remember things, I like to create acronyms or other pneumonic devices. I find it helps a lot. The High C's cover a series of affirmations that all begin with the letter C. These C's are characteristics I wish to continue developing. Perhaps you would like to try it out. If so, here are my High C's:

"I am caring, confident, courageous, calm, curious, conscientious, and celebratory of others."

I could write an entire book on this sentence—and I may one day. I chose the High C's as an affirmation because they cover many aspects of life that I would like to grow and improve. Let's look at each of the High C's individually. I think you'll see how they will impact most aspects of your life.

I am caring. Well, this one is a biggie! It's extremely important to care for others. This can be displayed with many people and in many ways. Think about the people you care about. Your loved ones, family and friends, and those in your company and your community. Do you care about others? I mean *really care*. Or do you approach life only thinking about how others will be able to serve you?

Caring about others will lead to fulfilling relationships in which all can benefit. Treating others as a means to an end can lead to riches, but they will be empty riches and often lead to a rather lonely existence.

One thing I've struggled with is *showing others* that I care. In the past, based on some experiences in my life, I have withheld caring behaviors for fear of being labeled as less manly or even a kiss-ass. But that mindset is so dumb! I have no excuses. Nowadays, I let people know that I care, even if that little voice inside my head raises concern. My rule is: If it comes from a place of love or caring, I shall say or do it. This includes giving constructive feedback, as true caring also means we can look someone in the eye and share things they may not want to hear but which we know will be helpful for them. This requires a certain level of our next C: confidence.

I am confident. Please hear me out. A huge gap between major success and mediocrity is the gap between knowing what to do and actually taking the action necessary to do it. Taking action starts with a level of confidence in what you are doing. Don't have it? Then go get it. Do it by studying, practicing, and then trying! I am confident, not cocky. There is a big difference. Cockiness comes from a place of ignorance and overcompensation. It comes from lacking knowledge, skills, or empathy. I look to the Dunning-Kruger Effect when considering the difference between cockiness and confidence.

ONE TO GROWN ON

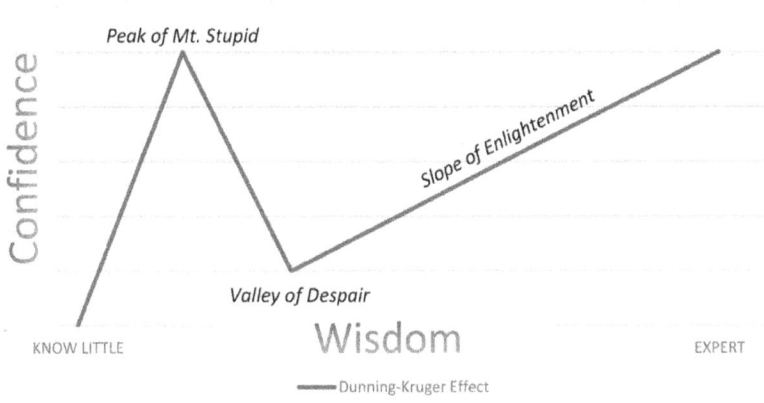

Following the chart from left to right, we see that people with some knowledge of a new subject generally overestimate their level of acumen and develop a false sense of confidence. In my mind, that is expressed as cockiness. We start sharing our "wisdom" with everyone, but at our core, we haven't fully grasped the depth or complexity of the subject. Also, we don't know what *we don't know*. I have been guilty of this. Perhaps I'm even guilty of it now, as I was only recently introduced to this phenomenon. It makes total sense though. Remember when people were acting like experts during the early stages of COVID-19? We were all telling each other what to do and acting like we knew what was going on. True confidence is gained after you come down from your mountain of cockiness and really take the time to understand a subject. This takes courage.

I am courageous. Courage is the true expression of our confidence. It is taking the necessary action in areas we believe we can make a difference. Courage sometimes introduces you to failure, from which more wisdom is born. In fact, some of the brightest minds in the world believe the only true failure is giving up. Everything else is simply part of the pathway to success. Knowledge without action is of limited value, and it takes courage to step out and be vulnerable.

One phrase I repeated over and over to myself back when I was struggling early in real estate was, "Do the difficult first." I knew that if I acted on the most important things I needed to do first, everything else about my day would fall in line and be productive. This is still a strategy and a mindset I employ today. And by the way, the pain of discipline is quickly replaced by a deep satisfaction when you accomplish tough things. But the pain of regret—the pain of knowing I could have done more if I'd had the courage to act—well, that pain lasts a long time. Sometimes it even lasts a lifetime. It takes courage to do the difficult first. And it takes a certain level of calmness.

I am calm. Wow, this one is important and tricky. Like everything else in life, strengths magnified or taken to extremes almost always become weaknesses. I pride myself on being the calm in the storm. However, this can lead to a perceived lack of empathy or elicit the question "Are you a robot?" from others. The key is not to ignore emotions or pretend they don't exist. Understand, though, that fueling fires and adding to situations that are already dramatic can have serious, even catastrophic, consequences. It is best to acknowledge whatever emotion(s) you are feeling, determine whether you are capable of communicating effectively, and then come up with ways to address the emotion(s). One of my mentors had some great advice here. "Kevin, whenever I feel things getting heated or speeding up, I take deep breaths and slow everything down: my thinking, my speaking, my responses." It's like the athlete that is so tuned in to the game that she can make great decisions as everything slows down around her. Getting caught up in the whirlwind is less effective.

ONE TO GROWN ON

It's also important to stay curious in life.

I am curious. Reading is a habit of mine, and it serves both me and others well. My father and grandfather are also avid readers. Many different subjects pique my interest, my favorites of which are leadership, strategy, negotiations, sales, and psychology. One recurring trait attributed to leaders across many credible books and periodicals is curiosity. Curiosity is a desire to learn new things. To explore. Everyone on earth has a purpose, and so I believe there is something to learn from everyone.

Are you curious about things? If so, carve out some time each day to learn about your interests. Talk to people, join a club, and ask questions! Oh my goodness, I love asking questions! I wish I'd been as curious as I am now earlier in life. I was the person who would scoff at the other kids in class for asking questions of the teachers—especially when they would ask something right before the bell was about to ring! I even poked fun now and then at what I considered to be "stupid" questions. Once, at an Arby's drive-thru, a friend of mine asked, "How much is the 5 for 5 meal?" I erupted in laughter and replied, "Five dollars, asshole!" Sure, this example is extreme, and the question truly wasn't a bright one, but I will say the person who asked this question was and is eternally curious and asks hundreds of questions every week. He is on his way to billions, and that is not an exaggeration!

As I've become more curious, more focused on others, and more intentional with how I spend time with others, I've also become a better listener. My empathy has improved, and I've started to develop a higher level of conscientiousness.

I am conscientious. This takes a reduction in ego, a reduction in self-centeredness, and an increase in your awareness of those around you and their positioning in the environment. You will also tune in to how they are behaving. Not necessarily what they are saying, but how they are behaving. Picking up on subtle is a good start to improving conscientiousness.

Next, you will start asking questions that help you get to the root of matters and identify if there is anything you can do to assist others. Please hear this: In many cases, people will feel better simply by being heard and understood. Sometimes you will help fix something or give advice when asked, and other times you will just be there for someone who is going through a rough time. I promise this is a difficult, albeit important, lesson.

A high level of conscientiousness makes for really thoughtful gift giving too. Some people I know constantly amaze me with their ability to give little gifts that might not cost much but that have great meaning. Take Linda Sherrer, for example, the founder of a company I once worked for. She has an amazing ability to know her people and what drives them. She'll gift a cookbook here, a favorite pie there, a donation to a meaningful cause on someone's behalf. Or she'll simply give someone a well-placed and meaningful compliment or bit of advice. She is a pro at paying attention and making people feel good. She perfectly exemplifies conscientiousness and celebrating others.

Speaking of which, I am celebratory of others. This is contrary to how some of us are wired and how many of us were raised. When I think our family is spending a little too much time fawning over our son, I speak up. I do not want him to grow up thinking the entire universe revolves around him—it just isn't true, and it will set him up for failure. I want him to look upward for guidance and look outward to celebrate others. I can say that I am not there yet in my personal journey. I wake up every day and consider how might I benefit someone personally and professionally. Or I ponder how I can make someone else feel valued and good about themselves. Although when the day gets hectic, sometimes my inner ego takes over and I find myself missing opportunities to do so. Thankfully, I believe that mistakes and missed opportunities are learning processes. And I know that improvement is tantamount to success. Which, by the way, is also a journey and not a destination.

When you develop yourself in these "High C" areas, you will become a better connector with people, which will lead to stronger relationships. This has not always been easy for me. In fact, it is something I still work on to this day—especially when it comes to curiosity and active listening. I am constantly trying to get better at listening *to understand* versus listening *to respond*.

When our son Elliott was about to turn four, he taught me something about conscientiousness. One morning before I took him to school, he asked if he could bring his little toy lizard with him. Lizzie, he calls her. I tried to discourage it and told him that small toys like that could get lost. He persisted, so I let him win our negotiation. Sure enough, when I picked him up from school later that day, Lizzie was nowhere to be found. He was trying to convince the teacher to help him look for her, but the teacher was distracted by the other kids. So I rushed him out the door with a comment similar to, "I told you so," and off we went.

When Jessica got home, I overheard Elliot telling her about losing Lizzie. I again jumped in to help him understand the lesson learned. I said it was important to take care of things that he brings to school so he doesn't lose them.

Eventually I forgot about it, and we moved on to dinner and playing a couple games. But before bed, he really started acting up. I mean he was being mean, refusing to do what we asked, and hollering. Acting up, acting out. The whole nine yards.

With my frustration rising, I tried to handle it using my CALM approach (outlined in detail later in the book). I took a deep breath in, and out. Then I sat on the edge of his bed and asked a question that is important in many, many different situations, "Buddy, you don't seem yourself. Is there something you want to talk about?"

He bursts into tears. Seriously, they were streaming down his face. "I lost my Lizzie! I need my Lizzie! I miss my Lizzie!" He cried and cried.

Suddenly I was fighting back tears. We talked about Lizzie. I listened to him and offered my empathy. Finally, we hugged.

Something that seemed so meaningless to me earlier—something that I had casually brushed aside as a life lesson—was eating him up inside. It was so important to him, but I hadn't given him the chance to express it. Wow. It's hard to explain this story even to this day. It still makes me tear up.

The story has a good ending, however. Lizzie was located the next day!

Get intentional with your programming:

1. Write this statement down 20 times a day for 30 days: "I am caring, confident, courageous, calm, curious, conscientious, and celebratory of others."
2. Pick one of the C's and visualize what it is and the results you might achieve by adopting the behavior.
3. Commit to displaying one or two of these characteristics during the day.

ONE TO GROWN ON

Share a personal affirmation in our online community (learn more at https://momentorsllc.com/one-to-grow-on-community/).

To start your journey, check out the appendix for a list of other affirmations I've used over the years. You don't *need* to use any of these—the point is to figure out what is important to you and in line with your values, then make your own affirmations. Some people also record their voice and listen to themselves while going for a walk or jog. Try different things, and then watch the results happen over time. Just as literal seeds planted in a garden take time to germinate, mental seeds will take time to develop into measurable results.

The point:

1. Focusing on the High C's will make your life more fulfilling and provide great benefits for the people around you. If you change your world, the goodness inside you can spread to others. The results will amaze you.
2. Ever feel down, nervous, anxious, or afraid? That's likely your ego at work. Start thinking about what you can do to serve others. In doing so, you will see your ego diminished.

Three more to explore:

Smart Talk by Lou Tice
Secrets of the Millionaire Mind by T. Harv Eker
The Law of Divine Compensation by Marianne Williamson

KEVIN M. WAUGAMAN

Read Our Blog on Powerful Self-Programming

---

[1] Michelle M. Lee, Kate M. Turetsky, and Julie Spicer, "Cognitive, Social, Physiological, and Neural Mechanisms Underlying Self-affirmation: An Integrative Review," *Yale Review of Undergraduate Research in Psychology*, Columbia University, 2017.

RIGHT ACTIONS LEAD TO STRONG RESULTS

The shower scene

Chances are you know the most valuable and important things you must do at your job. I bet you know the right attitude to bring and where to focus your time and energy. The same can probably be said of your personal life. Pay attention to your loved ones. Be present when you are with others. Make fitness and health a priority. Don't let distractions block out what matters most.

Doing the right thing consistently and with intention can be extremely difficult! Why? Because discipline is hard, and distractions are often really fun! But they are also more expensive than you realize. It's time to prioritize right actions and then bring your best to these things.

To say my financial situation was bad in the early 2000s would be an understatement. I had left a decent job in financial services in 2005 to pursue a real estate career. It seemed like a great idea at the time—there were lots of people who could help me and tons of money to make along the way. But there were also many challenges.

And oh yeah, I also bought my first home (a condo) in 2005. Brilliant! This was exactly at the height of the market, and immediately before the Great Recession. I was already in credit card debt (more on that topic in the chapter called Opportunity Cost and the Credit Card Crisis) but was making progress on my payments. The market in Stuart, Florida, was still okay and I was training and getting ready for the windfall of income that was forthcoming. The owner of the company was predicting dark times ahead, but he was the only one saying it. And I didn't know him well enough yet to trust his voice over all the others.

By the middle of 2007, I had muddled through with a few sales and was growing concerned because the velocity of traffic was seemingly screeching to a halt for even the more experienced agents. People were starting to panic. If you were around and remember the financial crisis, you understand how bad things were going to be.

To pay the bills back in my early days while the market was in shambles, I burned through my savings and 401K. I also eventually started racking up even more credit card debt. To this day, I am still grateful for the fact I wasn't married with children while going through that financial crisis.

One day, late in the year, my water was cut off while I was taking a shower. The utilities company, it turns out, is apparently more willing to serve those who pay their bills. If you have ever been in a situation like this, you know how completely demoralizing it is.

There was one other issue, too: I had a meeting scheduled at the office that morning with a prospective client. Obviously, I needed to bathe! I scrounged and collected as much change as I could find around my home and then drove to Publix with empty water jugs. Next I filled those jugs up, drove home, and finished taking a shower by dumping them over my head. Luckily I lived in the warmth of South Florida at the time. If I'd lived somewhere colder, dumping what felt like frigid water on my body would have been much worse.

As I was completing this exercise, I made a promise to myself and my future family: I will never put myself in this situation again.

Notice something in the above example: I took ownership of the problem and *did not* blame external circumstances. I knew I'd made my own bed. Why?

First, I'd made myself into a professional student. Except I wasn't getting paid to be a student. I convinced myself that I needed to know everything before I did anything. I took class after class. There is nothing wrong with learning, but unless you are a paid researcher, that learning needs to be followed by practice and then action. Two items were at play here: I was too comfortable in my comfort zone, and I feared stepping outside of it and making mistakes. When you evaluate how you spend your time, what are the things you might do less of or eliminate? These should be things that aren't moving the needle for you.

Second, as a salesperson, I would often latch on to prospects and spend all my time working on them instead of continuing to cultivate new relationships. Once a connection was made, it was more within my comfort zone to nurture (or in some cases suffocate) a relationship than to develop a new one. I was like Tommy Boy with his precious little pet. (Find this on YouTube if you have no idea what I'm talking about.) So, what might you increase in your daily approach to get outside of your comfort zone? Trust me, getting outside of your comfort zone can open a world of possibilities.

Finally, once I found a big fish prospect, I tried only to hit a grand slam. I forgot about trying for singles and doubles along the way. What about you? Do you get wrapped up in dreaming about huge opportunities? That's okay. But it is also important to continue to do the things that cultivate new opportunities of all sizes when you can.

Early in my career, I met a builder at an open house who told me he wanted to build waterfront condominiums in Stuart. I got excited and then proceeded to spend hours trying to find the right location, speaking with owners and other agents about assembling the land, and envisioning what the final product would look like. And yes, I also calculated my potential commission on the initial land sales and all the finished units I would sell after. Now, again, trying to hit the grand slam is okay. But you *need* to also hit those singles and doubles along the way. When the grand slam is a swing and a miss (in this case, the market changed and the builder changed his mind) and you haven't been collecting those singles and doubles, your batting average plummets to .000. I've seen this over and over again with agents and clients. Putting too many eggs in one basket means something devastating can happen. This "grand slam" approach has run many agents right out of the business.

Eventually, I realized there are many things within my control. Call it Triple A: Attitude, Activities, and the Adjustments we make. My attitude was actually okay back then, but my activity was slacking. In real estate and other sales jobs, it is possible to keep extremely busy while focusing on tasks that are on the periphery. Sending sales postcards, emails, newsletters, and social media posts out are all great, but they are not the most effective. For the most productive salespeople and leaders, the rubber still meets the road with face-to-face, voice-to-voice, and other personalized communication. Everything else augments these methods of communication because they are less risky and more comfortable.

That was where I was living.

On the way to the office on that cold-shower day, I knew I needed to make a change. I began telling myself every day that I would "Do the difficult first." This became my mantra, and I repeated it each morning. In real estate sales, the difficult part was keeping the day-to-day focus on prospecting for new business. This process required having face-to-face and voice-to-voice interactions with people. This meant I had to get to know a bunch of strangers, as I didn't know many people when I moved back to my hometown of Stuart. It also meant I would be receiving some direct rejection.

I got to work. I devised a plan to attack expired listings (what happens to a home after it is on the market unsuccessfully for a period of time with another real estate agent) and even enlisted the support of a top agent in the office to partner on some opportunities. My literal hunger for success combined with his track record led to a winning strategy. We started listing property, and I went from near-last in my firm in individual agent productivity to second (only to him) in 2008. That was only my third full year in the business. And it was one of the worst years in the history of real estate sales.

2008 was my most successful year in real estate sales. And what was the market doing at the time? Plummeting. It would have been easy for me to blame the market and give up. I even toyed with the idea of a return to my prior world. But my determination and competitive nature kicked in. I was focused on succeeding. Once I paired my new attitude with taking risks and doing the right things (activities), I was off to the races.

This set the stage for a rewarding long-term career in real estate. I eventually decided leadership was the right path for me. I took over as VP of Sales, then moved back to Jacksonville to be Managing Broker for a flagship office. And then I became the VP of Core Services for that company prior to taking the reins as CEO.

To become more effective with your time:

1. Make a list of the three things you do in your job that are the most important. Do the same for your personal life.
2. Commit to spending a little more time on those things each day. Schedule the time. Treat it like a non-negotiable appointment!
3. Every week, schedule the most important things for the following week on your calendar. The most important things in your professional and personal life go on the calendar first.

One principle at work here is the Pareto Principle, or the rule of 20/80. This principle states that 80% of your results will come from 20% of your efforts. If you can pay attention and learn what your key activities are, you can do more of those things and reduce your time spent on the other activities. Delegate the activities that give you less return, stop doing them if

> If you can pay attention and learn what your key activities are, you can do more of those things and reduce your time spent on the other activities.

possible, or hire someone else to do them if you don't currently have the support.

The point:

1. Focus on what you KNOW are the most important aspects of your job and your relationships. Ensure these are things you can control.
2. There is almost always a way to win in spite of external circumstances.
3. Invest time each day cultivating current relationships and developing new ones.

Three more to explore:

The Compound Effect by Darren Hardy
The Power of Full Engagement by Jim Loehr and Tony Schwartz
Win the Day by Mark Batterson

Read Our Blog On Right Actions Strong Results

IDEAS ARE CHEAP, EXECUTION IS GOLD

One bite at a time

I always thought the question "How do you eat an elephant?" was a bit odd. When I first heard the question in my youth, my reply was, "You don't!"

Since I enjoy smoking meats on my Big Green Egg, let's rephrase the question to: "How do you eat a delicious Texas-style brisket?" The answer? One bite at a time.

Many of the great things in life that we want to tackle can seem overwhelming. Even some of the smaller things we want to accomplish can appear that way. So, we need to break things down into smaller, more manageable tasks. One bite at a time.

When I was building a real estate career into the teeth of the Great Recession, I had quite a hard time getting started. At the time, I had no idea that overcoming these early challenges would launch me on a 20+ year journey of successful sales and leading teams and companies through major market shifts and a pandemic. As I mentioned in the last chapter, one of the strategies I employed early on to break out of my funk was to connect with sellers whose listings had recently expired. When a real estate agent lists a home, there is an agreement with the seller that stipulates how long the agent has to sell the home. Upon the end of this term, the property "expires" from the market. This prospecting activity was not the most fun endeavor when I initially took it on, as it required cold calling and contacting people who were already irritated by real estate agents like me. The result was that a property would expire and then 30 agents would call, email, text, or mail information to the homeowners. As you might expect, some of these folks were pretty annoyed when I got them on the phone—because they'd already spoken to several other agents before me.

Whilst at the bottom of my financial barrel, I decided that listing and selling expired homes was the fastest way to get results. And then I got started. I sat down at my computer, pulled up the Multiple Listing Service (MLS)—our main source of data on properties—and created a list of 100 properties that had expired over the past month. And then I ... sat. And looked at the list. And clicked on the links. And read all the comments. And pulled up the tax records. And grabbed a snack, and walked the dog, and sat back down. And read some more, thinking, *Hmmm, I don't know much about that neighborhood.* And Googled the neighborhood, then read about the neighborhood. And daydreamed about the neighborhood and future home ownership, then got in my car and drove through the neighborhood.

Wait—what was my problem?

If you guessed procrastination caused by fear of failure, you'd be partially right. I hate to admit it today, but I was incredibly stagnant those first two years of my career. I thought I needed to know everything and develop a level of comfort before I could do what needed to be done. But that thinking was all wrong. The key is to study, practice, and then take action! Then, after you make some mistakes, you can learn what to do differently. Next, take action again! In that action is where the real learning happens. It's how you get good and then great.

The other part of the problem was that I didn't have a system. I was overwhelmed by the thought of prospecting and taking listings, which ultimately amounted to my fear of yes! Crazy, right? Not really! I figured that if someone said yes, I would have to visit them and give a listing presentation. Then what? Was I ready for that? What if they asked me a question I didn't know the answer to? Would I look foolish? This thought process went on and on for me. It was painful.

I finally got good at listing expired properties when I developed a system for it. I broke the big project down into manageable pieces to better execute. My process looked something like this:

1. During the last week of the month, I would pull a list of every property that was set to expire over the next month.
2. Next, I'd identify A/B/C levels of desire to take that listing five days prior to the first day of the month.
3. I would go take pictures of all the "A" potentials prior to first day of month. (And I would always save the photos, because even if a property was relisted by another agent, the opportunity may again come in the future.)
4. I prepared a stack of MLS pages in order of date that expired before the 1st of the month.
5. Every day before 8:30 a.m., I would review the stack and confirm whether that day's expired listings came off the market or were relisted.

6. Next, I prepared packages for the expired listings and dropped the photos in the materials for the "A" section before noon that day.
7. If the listing was an A, I'd drive over and hand-deliver the package on the first day of expiration.
8. If it was a B, I'd call the owner on the first day of expiration by 5:00 p.m.
9. If it was a C, I'd mail out a seller packet on the first day of expiration by 5:00 p.m.
10. I'd set appointments for when I could make connections. Or I would get permission for a follow-up call on day three.
11. I would file an MLS sheet in the appropriate folder for follow-up dates.
12. Then I would put a handwritten note in the mail for anyone that took the time to answer the call or the door.
13. On day three of expiration, I'd conduct a follow-up call.
14. On day five of expiration, I'd conduct a follow-up regarding my mailers.
15. On day 10 of expiration, I'd send out another handwritten note.
16. On day 30, if the property wasn't relisted, I'd send a monthly note. I'd continue doing this for one year.

The key here is not the process itself. Instead, I want you to note how specific I made these smaller steps. Let's pull this apart so you can see how it applies to any process. First, you must prioritize your options to determine which tasks require the most effort and energy. For me, the location of the home and price were key points. Next, you must be clear on timelines so you know what to do each day, week, or hour depending on the size of the endeavor. Some bigger projects might be broken into monthly deliverables. In that case, you can still move key steps to your calendar and allocate specific time to each task. You can move on to the next task when you hit your marks along the way. This helps you minimize distractions and stay focused on the smaller steps you need to accomplish. Finally, you can follow up and report back to the proper people when the tasks and project are finished.

Also, I got my listing process down, so I knew exactly what to do when someone agreed to let me come preview the home and discuss the listing. This started happening more and more frequently as I improved my delivery. Now, I certainly could have studied and practiced another year before I actually started calling and knocking on doors. But that would have gotten me nowhere. There is something about the emotion and feeling of the actual engagement and connection that helps us grow and get better. You just cannot get that in a classroom.

Once I had the process down and started picking up the phone, I got better. At first, I was bad. I stammered and fumbled through conversations, I got hung up on, I hung up on some people. Hilarious, right? I finally had people on the phone and yet I was rushing *them* off! And then, gradually, I started really learning and gaining confidence. Eventually, I mastered the skill. How? With perseverance. You know what I really learned? To put away the scripts. Instead, I decided to be honest, bring some humor to the situation when possible, listen to the other person, provide empathy, and offer something of value. I started creating a structure for the call—not a script, but structure. I broke the calls down into three sections, and then I gave myself complete flexibility within the framework. In the case of the expired listings, this process would look like this:

1. **Greeting:** "Hello and good afternoon. Is this Mr. Jones? This is Kevin Waugaman with Premier Realty Group. How are you, sir?"
2. **Questions to ask:** "Did I catch you at a good time? I noticed your property came off the market. Is it still available for sale? When would be a good time for me to preview it? Why do you think it didn't sell? Why are you selling? What was your experience like during the process? What do you think your plans are going forward?"
3. **Next steps:** "I'd be happy to offer a complimentary evaluation. Would you find value in our latest market report? I'm happy to drop it off."

Look at that call structure. It can work for any type of call. You can add in more rapport-building questions, or you can change the questions and next steps to suit your network/industry. The structure works regardless. Don't over-script yourself—it comes off as less than authentic and can turn people off.

Whether you are working on a project individually or as a team, the completion is always more likely to occur when you take the end result you desire and break it down into small, manageable steps with deadlines for each one. When the important things go on your calen-

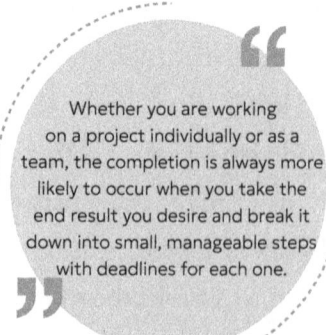

Whether you are working on a project individually or as a team, the completion is always more likely to occur when you take the end result you desire and break it down into small, manageable steps with deadlines for each one.

dar, you need to treat them as you would an appointment. In other words—no distractions! Even if it's an appointment with yourself to do some sales prospecting, write your book, or develop a new training program, you can't let distractions get in the way.

There is also something called Parkinson's Law of Time Management, which states that work will expand or contract to fill the time you've allotted for it. If you don't set aside time for the task, chances are it will fill your time until your next scheduled appointment. And it will generally take longer than it should. But if you set a time and are on a deadline, the work often gets done faster and better!

This has become more of a strength in my life, with practice, over the years. When someone I'm coaching finds themselves overwhelmed, I pull out an old-fashioned legal pad and start asking questions to help them discover the path forward. After we discuss the issue and reach the point where the rubber meets the road, I ask, "What do you think needs to happen first? Next? How about after that? And then?" I write it all out in step-by-step form and then we both assess what we've written. In most cases, this simplified process will reveal the best answer from the person who was overwhelmed.

To improve your ability to execute:

1. Pick something on your life list that you want to accomplish this year. Break it down into actionable steps that you can accomplish on a timeline.
2. Think of something you do weekly or monthly—something that you haven't attached a process to. Break it down into steps with references to resources (so someone else

would be able to accomplish it in your absence). Along the way, you may find a more effective way to accomplish the task. Also, you will ensure that you know what steps to take each time.
3. Use your calendar and block out time for these activities. The important things on your to-do list deserve a spot on your calendar. Over time, you will improve and gain a deep understanding of how long things actually take.
4. Share your goal and some of the steps you are taking in our One To Grow On community at www.MomentorsLLC.com. Maybe you'll inspire someone!

Make sure you leave enough flexibility to bring your personality, focus on the needs of others, and ensure these processes don't become ruts. You want to be able to have fun along the way and let the systems and processes evolve over time.

You will find you get more done and that you are more effective if you develop processes.

The point:

1. When you are trying to accomplish something, start by breaking it down into small, manageable steps with deadlines attached.
2. Anything you need to do on a constant basis will benefit from having a process defined. The process can be flexible.

Remember, Henry Ford said, "Nothing is particularly hard when you divide it into small jobs."

ONE TO GROWN ON

Three more to explore:

Execution by Larry Bossidy and Ram Charan

The 4 Disciplines of Execution by Chris McChesney, Sean Covey, and Jim Huling

Time Management From the Inside Out by Julie Morgenstern

Our Blog on Execution

YOUR BEST TODAY WILL SET UP YOUR BEST TOMORROW

Hard work and commitment pay off in many ways

How do you approach your day? Are you proactive or reactive? Growing or shrinking? It all starts with your Morning Kickstart and programming. After that, it's about doing the right things, executing, and bringing your best day in and day out. If you slip up—and we all do, because we are human and very imperfect—how quickly can you get back on track? These are important questions. Habit development and payoff take time. Author James Clear said, "Habits are not a finish line to be crossed, they are a lifestyle to be lived."

Sometimes bringing your best means keeping your head down and your eyes on the job. Sometimes it means stepping back and having an important one-on-one conversation with a colleague. Sometimes it means having a challenging conversation with a boss or employee. But to me, bringing your best often means doing the difficult first. When you tackle the tough tasks early in the day or week, you are setting yourself up to have a momentum that will carry you forward with great force. Regardless of the outcome, you will appreciate the fact that you're taking the challenge head on. Remember: Your ability to overcome challenges and provide solutions directly impacts your ability to earn an income.

One of the first jobs I ever had was as a dining room attendant at the Café on the Green at the Sawgrass Marriott in Ponte Vedra Beach, Florida. In other words, I was a busboy.

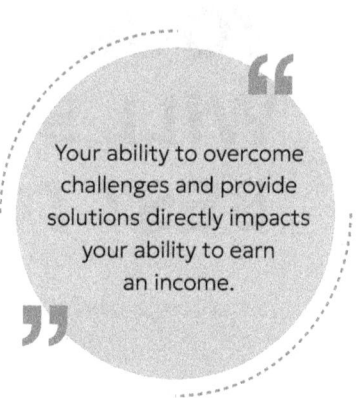

"Table 22 just got sat, Dan. You got water? I'll grab the bread!"

"Let's do it."

There were two busboys that summer—Dan and I—and we became partners in crime and good friends. Now, a busboy job is probably considered by many to be mundane and low level. They do not see it as a real opportunity. But Dan and I, somehow, developed a passion for the job. I think this passion had to do with the friendship we developed. We made a game out of it—to see how fast we could greet patrons and provide water and bread for each table. We didn't divide up the restaurant like management asked us to. Instead, we shared the entire space, one on bread and the other on water, with both of us turning the tables when they were vacated. We had it down and were a well-oiled busboy machine. We truly approached the job with a level of engagement rarely matched. At the end of each evening, we got tipped out by the servers and split the tips.

It would have been a boring job if not for our bond. Making it fun was important. We developed great relationships with the staff, including the managers, chefs, servers, security guards, and the hostess. We poked fun at everyone and didn't take ourselves too seriously. How could we? Once, we went up to the fourth floor of the hotel and dropped cloth napkins down like mini parachutes to see if we could land one on the hostess. It turned out—much to her surprise—that we could!

This "bring your best every day" approach allows you to make the most out of any circumstance. And with the relationships you form, it is a great way to set yourself up for future success.

There is something to be said about making today your masterpiece no matter where you are in life. Why? Because it will set you up for a better tomorrow. Hate your job? Bring your best today and every day anyway, because I promise it is better than doing just enough to get by. Work hard. Help others get better. Greet everyone with respect. Because the truth is this: The better I am today, the better I become tomorrow, and the better my circumstances will be. I will develop better habits and better relationships. I will set a good example for others. I will develop the habit of bringing my best each and every day. There is so much good that comes from this, and it will absolutely strengthen character. When the opportunity to start an impactful business came knocking, I was more prepared. I had developed incredible relationships over the years and was ready to win at the current opportunity.

This level of resilience requires a strong mindset. I've had a few jobs that I hated, and I've handled some poorly and others superbly. Doing just enough to get by was sort of my approach to college and my first jobs out of college. My priorities and values were not aligned, and work and personal growth were not part of the equation.

But I managed to get through it, and when my first leadership job presented itself to me, I was ready for it and had a much better mindset.

During my five years in that role, we grew the company by a factor of almost double and hired some amazing people. It was a great experience for a while, but then some bumps in the road caused a bit of strife among the staff. The job became extremely challenging, and I felt out of alignment. It would have been very easy for me to leave or just do enough to get by until I had fulfilled my verbal five-year commitment.

But I didn't do that. Instead, I elevated my game. I became an expert mediator to resolve differences. I kept hiring and training great people. My mission? To leave the place far better than I found it—for the benefit of everyone. And I accomplished that mission. In fact, if you look at the company today, many of the top people were hired and trained while I was there, and some of my best hires took place during my last few months on the job. The work became more challenging, but I did it to the absolute best of my ability and would do it again under the same circumstances. Considering the work environment, it was a major accomplishment.

As parents, we want the best for our children. When we are traveling to a school play or a sports game or soccer practice, we ask our children about the approach they are going to take. And we want to hear two things: "I plan to have fun and bring my best effort." That's a good approach to life, yes?

Bring your best to your job even if it's not what you want to do.

Bring your best during your family time even if you are tired.

Bring your best to your community and your friendships.

Bring your best to your spiritual life.

Simply put, bringing your best today sets you up for the best tomorrow.

What is the alternative? Do just enough to get by? Or worse—don't do enough and get fired? Or divorced? Bringing your best will also feed back into your self-confidence and your ability to focus more on being present where you are. Let's explore this idea for a moment.

I mentioned there was a period during my real estate sales career when I had one foot out the door. I was considering going back to my former employer. I was only partially engaged, working a few hours here and there in an attempt to get something going. I most definitely was not "all in." On top of that, I was never fully present with my girlfriend or with other hobbies and interests, and I wasn't sleeping very well. Something was always in the back of my mind, distracting me. And I had a serious problem with my level of engagement and focus. My lack of effort was making me feel guilty!

Once I started focusing on all the strategies laid out in this book, I got my act together and started firing on all cylinders. Everything changed. I was more present, I was able to enjoy time off and vacations more, I slept better, and I gained confidence. And as a result, I was able to secure a series of big promotions over the years in the real estate industry. It was all because I got back into the habit of bringing my best every day no matter what the external circumstances were.

To bring your best:

1. Evaluate your level of daily engagement on a scale of 1-10 in these key areas:
   a. Family
   b. Occupation
   c. Recreation
   d. Body and health
   e. Education and personal growth
   f. Spirituality

2. For anything that scores below a seven, consider what you need to do to level up your game. Write it down and commit to getting a little better each day.
3. Try and come up with ways to make things more fun. In the case of relationships, discover how to strengthen your bonds.
4. Create habits that align with your objectives. Write them down and put them on your calendar.

Legendary NCAA hoops coach John Wooden used to say to his players, "Give me 100%. You can't make up for a poor effort today by giving me 110% tomorrow. You don't have 110%. You only have 100%, and that's what I want from you right now."

If you approach the day with less than your best—say 80%—that 20% difference from your best is lost forever.

Please make it a point to try and become the absolute best at whatever you do! If you take your energy and put it to good use for the benefit of others, the world will be a much better place. Whatever makes your heart sing, go all in and try to become the best of the best—the top 10% in your field. For some of you, you won't be satisfied until you reach the top 1%. God bless you!

Iconic musician and performer Justin Timberlake said, "Yesterday is history. Tomorrow's a mystery." (Okay, this quote most likely came from someone before JT. But the takeaway is clear: Our focus should be on today and how we show up. Chances are you can better shape the mystery of tomorrow into something appealing to you if you remain focused.)

Do you remember the chapter on our Morning Kickstart and starting the day off right? It's all about habits and your daily agenda.

ONE TO GROWN ON

By now, hopefully you have added some activities to your Morning Kickstart and are on your way to developing it.

Next, it's time to start layering daily and weekly habits on top of your Morning Kickstart. Doing so will help you make your life as fulfilling as it deserves to be. If this seems daunting, it might just be. Take the ideas from the chapter "One Bite at a Time and Execute" and just start small.

The point:

1. When you bring your best to your spiritual life, your personal life, and your professional life, you set yourself up for a better tomorrow.
2. When combined with affirmations, you will begin to attract positivity into your life and take the proper action steps towards your desired outcomes.

Three more to explore:

The Slight Edge by Jeff Olson
Atomic Habits by James Clear
Today Matters by John Maxwell

KEVIN M. WAUGAMAN

Our Most Recent Blog

GROW YOUR SALES ABILITY, GROW YOUR INFLUENCE

Sales skills are relevant for everyone

Whether you are in the sales industry or not, you are in sales. Every day you are selling yourself, selling an idea to someone, or selling something you own to someone else. Sales is everywhere! Plus, people are always trying to sell you something, aren't they? And you know what? It's okay! That's simply the world we live in. So, best to master some concepts and get the best possible outcomes, right? I have a great deal of experience in sales, and I will do my best to relate many valuable stories into digestible material for you, the reader. Here is one of those stories.

The ad in the paper read, "Earn $2,400 per week setting up displays! Learn more at D and D Distributors on Saturday at 2:00 p.m." It was the summer between my sophomore and junior years in college, and that was an extreme amount of money for a kid like me in the '90s. I showed up with a couple of friends, walked into a large room that accommodated about 50 people, and sat near the back since the front rows had already filled up. The room was bubbling with anticipation and folks wondering, "Will I be chosen for the work?" "How will I win one of the spots?" and most importantly, "What exactly *is* the work?!"

Around 2:30, a sweaty, stocky man lugging a big box burst through the doors. I thought: *Now we are getting somewhere. This box must contain the contents of the displays we'll be setting up for $2,400 per week.*

And then, suddenly, the man stopped in the front of the room and tore into the box with great gusto. When he stepped away from his work for the great reveal, we saw before us a Kirby vacuum cleaner.

Naïve as I was, I started thinking "No problem! I can set these things up all day, every day for $2,400 per week." But what I would soon come to learn was that "setting up displays" meant:

1. Riding around in a van all day with four other "display-setter-uppers"
2. Taking turns knocking on random doors
3. Convincing an unsuspecting person to let me into their home
4. Assembling a Kirby vacuum cleaner (the "display" part of the job)
5. Vacuuming a portion of their home to show them what filthy animals they were
6. Selling them a $1,600 machine to reduce their filthiness
7. Doing this entire process successfully four times per week to earn the $2,400

Looking back, it was a good lesson in that adage of: "If it seems too good to be true, then it probably is too good to be true." Most

ONE TO GROWN ON

things in life that are rewarding require a level of work—at least initially—that aligns with the reward.

No surprise, my friends bolted. None of them wanted to take on the challenge. But I did. I wanted to give it a try. The company was a Berkshire Hathaway (Scott Fetzer Company) subsidiary, which I suppose gave the role some credibility in my mind.

Anyway, I didn't sell four units per week—I sold three units the entire summer. I particularly struggled because I refused to sell the product to people I thought didn't need it or couldn't afford it. Also, at first, I was really poor at the job. I was scared of knocking on doors, and I fumbled through every sales pitch.

I gained confidence as I progressed though, as one does with anything they set their mind to. I got pretty good towards the end of summer, which is when the sales started coming in. What an incredible lesson it was in communicating with people, earning a living through sales, and dealing with and moving on from rejection.

The big lesson here is that rejection is a part of life. If you don't know this yet, you will someday. The best advice I can give is to accept rejection, learn from it, and make adjustments where necessary. If you look at your rejections as learning opportunities, you will eventually learn to embrace them. If you place blame externally for rejections, you will miss out on the learning and growth that comes with each one.

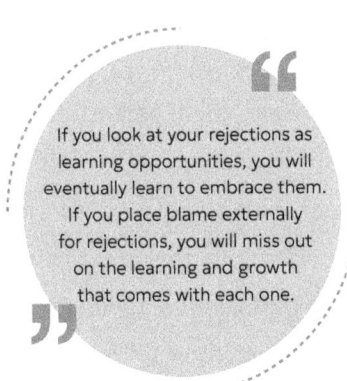

> If you look at your rejections as learning opportunities, you will eventually learn to embrace them. If you place blame externally for rejections, you will miss out on the learning and growth that comes with each one.

My next sales job was right out of college. I was answering phones as a client services rep for a mortgage company. My evolution from a vacuum cleaner salesman was well underway. Next, I moved into a financial advisory role working on small accounts, and then into real estate. At first, I listed and sold real estate. Then I developed an expertise of the craft over three years and started teaching sales skills to other agents.

I am going to teach you a sales process that has worked for me over the years and for the many agents I have trained. It is simple, but extremely effective. But before I get into that, please hear this: The attitude you adopt will make or break your sales success. I have seen attitude beat out acumen (your practical knowledge of a subject or your craft) time and time again. Now, for the benefit of your potential clients, I encourage you to develop the skills associated with whatever you are selling. Just think of this other Triple A acronym I created: Attitude + Acumen + Action = really good results.

Enhance acumen via:

1. Study
2. Practice
3. Discussion for feedback (especially from other experts in your field)
4. Implementation

And then please remember that sales is influence, and you want to use your sales skills for good. Ensure your objectives always align with those you wish to serve. Otherwise, you will find yourself manipulating your people instead of positively influencing them. And that is not a good way to build a long-term relationships.

Now, time to discuss that process. This will help you prepare for any meeting in which you are trying to bring a certain level of influence to the table. These are my words, but I am sure you will see many variations that sound familiar. This process works for any situation in which you are trying to influence someone in your personal or professional life.

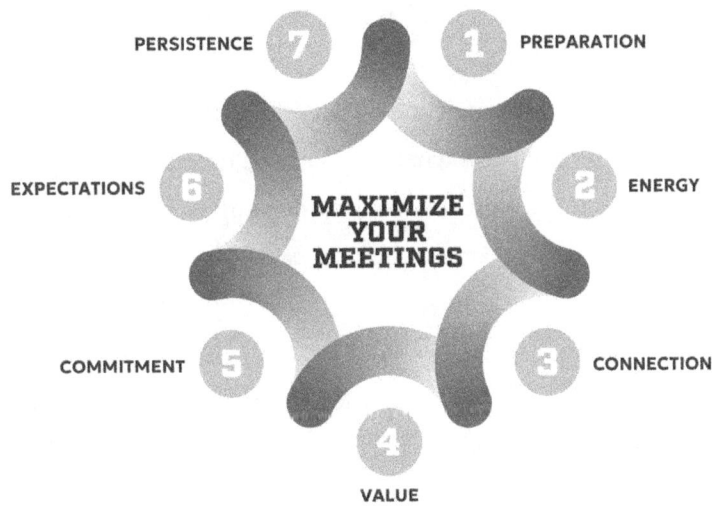

Here's a bit more insight into these seven attributes and what to consider when dealing with each one:

1. Preparation: Know your topic/audience and prepare great questions to ask them.
2. Energy: BRING IT. The most important traits in this regard are confidence, gratitude, and empathy.
3. Connection: Listen and care about the answers to your questions. Ask follow-up questions to gain clarity.
4. Value: What's in it for them? What makes your offering different? What options can you create to solve their challenge?

5. Commitment: Agree to move forward with an agreement or plan a follow-up conversation.
6. Expectations: Get clear on what happens next. Answer when applicable who/what/when/where/why/and how.
7. Persistence: This can be a good trait in sales *when handled professionally*. You don't want to come off as pushy, though.

As you progress through the sales cycle, it may be necessary to return to step one and assess whether you need to make adjustments.

Now, let's break this process down using a real job-seeking example. This way, you can see the process at play in other areas of life.

When I moved to Jacksonville in 2014, friends of my family connected me to Christy Budnick for an interview as a broker at a flagship office for Berkshire Hathaway HomeServices Florida Network Realty. I had no idea at the time that this was the beginning of a ten-year journey that would culminate in my being CEO of the company. I do believe that the beginning of a relationship is important, and I took our initial conversations and meetings very seriously. Here's how I approached this interview using the seven steps above.

Preparation: This part is fairly straightforward. I reviewed the company website and news, studied the local real estate market, learned about the key people at the company, met with people familiar with the company to ask questions, and prepared a list of my own questions—thoughtful questions—that I meant to ask during the interview. This step gave me a higher level of confidence walking through the door.

Energy: This is the part that makes or breaks the first impression. You definitely want to read the room. Not all people are attracted to high charisma and someone who is super talkative. In my experience, a beneficial approach to all meetings typically includes a combination of confidence in self, gratitude for the meeting, and empathy for the challenges the other person is facing. This is exactly the energy I brought to my interview. This step helped set us all at ease and prepared us for the next phase.

Connection: Remember the work we did in the preparation phase? Now is the time to put it to work. Ask questions. When appropriate, start with some non-work-related questions to break the ice. Care about the answers. Ask follow-up questions based on the responses. Take notes. Lean in and maintain eye contact. Confirm your understanding when appropriate. For this meeting, I had really good questions about the real estate market, the culture of the company, their perceived strengths and weaknesses, what their key challenges were, what I could do to help, the backgrounds of the people, and the history of the company. I already knew some of these answers from the website, but I knew it was valuable to hear it all straight from the source. This step helped us gain mutual likeability.

Value: Quite frankly—and I've seen this happen over and over again in all the hiring I've done—if the previous steps are handled appropriately, this doesn't become a sales job. This is now a mutual conversation about how we can work together and what value we bring to the table. That is exactly what happened in this interview. We got along so well that it seemed almost certain we would end up working together.

I did take some time, however, to build value. I did this by describing how my experience would help the office and company grow. I shared what I believed were unique attributes of my personality and my approach to sales and leadership. I shared some of the extracurricular activities I was involved in that had helped increase my skills and abilities. I shared with them my vision for what this office would grow to become and the culture I would create there. Everything I shared was essentially an answer to the challenges they'd described while outlining the position. This step helps differentiate you from others and may increase your compensation.

Commitment: This didn't happen on the spot, although I was told an offer would be made. It's always good to agree to, at the end of the meeting, whether we are moving forward or not. And if there are other options to consider, the protocol for following up should be specified. This step builds clarity.

Expectations: Once the agreement is made, it's time to cover the who/what/when/where/how and why of what happens next. In this example, we discussed the onboarding process, with whom I would be meeting, the topics we would discuss, timing for my introduction to the office, and what materials I would need to study in advance. It was all laid out beautifully. This step minimizes surprises and disappointment.

Persistence: This step was not necessary in the example I'm using. The flow took us quickly to an agreement. I will tell you, though, that there is nothing wrong with being persistent until you get a yes or a no. But you must be professional and respectful in your persistence.

How does this hit for you? Do you have a meeting coming up in which these steps would make a difference? Or maybe you have a committee or board meeting that you feel you can make a bigger impact on. Well, these steps can be applied to just about any meeting—and you will notice a big difference.

ONE TO GROWN ON

Whether you are in sales or simply want to increase your influence, you first must secure a prospect or have an audience willing to hear your message. Someone who will listen to you and hopefully have some sort of desire for what you are selling or trying to implement. There are many ways to set this up, and there are many marketing and sales books that tackle this subject—some better than others. I will give three pieces of advice here to get you started.

First, understand that your main objective is getting together for an in-person meeting. This is true especially when you are trying to influence someone on an important matter or there is potential conflict at stake. In the age of social media and text messages, there are several ways to succeed in influence and building relationships. But still, nothing replaces the connection of an in-person meeting.

Many of us overdo it in the connection phase by "selling"—over the phone, online, via text—before we have built the relationship. The key is to communicate your ability to solve a problem or create a win for the person you are trying to influence. This is done by being a person of integrity, providing great service, becoming a reliable source of information for your product or service, marketing and advertising, and ultimately provoking your potential client's curiosity.

Second, you should have a clear understanding of the benefits of your idea, product, service, method, or program and communicate it succinctly. If you are selling a product or a service, what are the competitive advantages (sometimes called unique selling propositions, or USPs)? How does it solve problems? How is it easier to use than other products?

When you are developing relationships and someone asks what you do, I suggest you use the following formula to secure an appointment. I'll use retargeting ad sales as an example:

1. Start with a question: "You know how when you are scrolling through social media the ads displayed there are tailor-made for you?"
2. Then a brief feature description: "We provide that technology. That way, your company can reach the community online that is most likely to purchase the product."
3. Followed with the benefit: "This drives added revenue while reducing the cost of client acquisition."

Third, know how to remove pressure whenever possible. Most of the time, our influence doesn't involve life or death matters. For real estate sales, the response might look something like this: "Kevin, I understand your service. It sounds really good. We're just not there yet. We don't want to waste your time." That is external dialogue. But the internal dialogue is this: "We are afraid of you. We think you are going to sell us something we don't want or need. This isn't going to be fun." Some people will recognize the value of your product or service but will not engage with you because they are afraid of something I call "sales discomfort." Here's the key: If relationships are important to you in sales, I would encourage you to remove the pressure and then honor it. "Mr. and Mrs. Jones, I am working with some who will write a contract today, and others who will be ready six months from now. The benefit of starting the process now is that we will better understand what you are looking for and have you that much more prepared in six months." This response is gold. And when you also use the seven-step meeting process I shared in this chapter, you will find that some are more ready to move forward than they thought. All it takes is a gentle attitude and no pressure from you.

Let's also add four rules of influence to help you along the way as you implement these concepts:

Rule #1: Ask Questions With a Passionate Intent to Understand

Do you ask questions to listen and understand? Or do you ask questions to respond? There is wisdom in the old saying that we have two ears to listen and only one mouth to speak, and therefore we should listen twice as much as we speak! But there is a challenge in this. When you listen, are you formulating your response while the other person is talking? If so, you have some work to do.

Admittedly, this has been a challenge for me. It is something I still work on. When someone speaks to me, my mind will start to wander, and I will start thinking of how to address that portion of what they said. The problem is that they are still talking while I'm doing that thinking! This can lead to some embarrassing moments. Ever ask someone a question even though they already addressed the topic in their last sentence? Their *last sentence*! Come on! It's so awkward! It's also a great recipe for harming your business relationships.

Recently Jessica and I were discussing an event she was preparing for, and I asked her what time it started on Friday. I also asked whether I needed to pick up Elliott from school.

"Where have you been?" she asked. Uh-oh, I thought. "I just said the event was moved to next week and Elliott will be with Grammy and Papa," she said. I was in trouble for that one!

You see, trying to think of a response while someone else is talking is a form of multi-tasking. And according to many studies out there, multi-tasking *does not work*. Your conscious brain is simply switching back and forth from one thing to the next, not doing both at the same time. Either the listening will suffer, or the thinking will. Or *both* will suffer. Focus on what the other person is saying and then be okay with taking a moment to collect your thoughts.

Put your whole person into listening. Lean forward and make eye contact. Take notes if appropriate. And then, when you're ready, ask for clarity by repeating key points back to the speaker. In some instances, what was said and what you heard were two different things. It is completely fine to ask if you heard someone right by sharing with them what *you heard*. "To make sure I am clear, is this what you meant …?"

If possible, try using open-ended questions to get the answers you need. This helps foster a connection and avoids making the discussion feel like an interrogation. For example, in real estate I get a ton of great information by asking the following questions of a potential buyer:

"Tell me about where you live now?"

"What do you love most about your current home?"

"What would you change?"

"How about the neighborhood?"

"What do you like to have in the near vicinity?"

And so on. You get the point. Based on this conversation, I will likely get a solid picture of what they want and need in a home without having to ask:

"How many bedrooms/bathrooms do you need?"

"What's your price range?"

"Your square footage requirements?"

This line of questioning is not fun. It makes people feel interrogated.

Ask great questions, then listen to them to understand and connect. Not to respond.

A note on relationships in general. Approach each person as a valuable individual. Ask questions to learn about them, and soon you will develop strong relationships and become so much more well-rounded, knowledgeable, and fun as a result.

Rule #2: Provide Options for the Solution

In the upcoming chapter on negotiations, I'll touch on the importance of options. Let's dive in a bit now, too, because the topic is important. You will be able to see the power of options from various angles as you work to help others get what they want.

Here is the key thing to ask yourself: Does your offering match up with what the person wants or needs? Or does it add some sort of value to them, only now they require a bit more discussion to fully understand that value? If so, proceed! If not, tell the truth and move on. If you are so "good at sales" that you can convince people to buy or do things that don't align with their objective, I would submit that you aren't using your influence in a responsible way. Think about the damage you'll inflict upon yourself over time with that approach. Will you have satisfied clients, friends, and family? How will the people you care about feel about you? In sales, will you get referrals and repeat business? Not a chance. On the flip side, being honest with people will help you develop a reputation as a go-to person in your field.

You've gathered enough information through good questions and listening. Now it is time to lay out the options. A couple tips here:

1. Know your product and service really well. This helps you build confidence, which is a must. When an actor doesn't know their lines, it produces stage fright. And when a salesperson doesn't fully know their product or service, it creates a similar type of fear. Which creates a sales drought.
2. Understand and communicate the benefits derived by the features. For instance, the car you're selling may have a state-of-the-art parking system and hands-free assisted driving. But you can't rely on the buyer to make the connection. Take it one step further. "This means stress-free parking. Also, the chances of an accident in a parking lot are greatly reduced." Lower stress and lower chance of an accident occuring. Those are the benefits.
3. Next, you must address potential concerns. Using the hands-free car example, many will be concerned about the potential of their car taking control. "Some may hesitate with this automation, but just know that the driver is able to override the car at any time. This allows you to make the same split-second decisions as you would in your current vehicle when necessary."

Lay out options if possible, including different feature sets, payment options, or service levels. This helps people make decisions based on relative value perception.

ONE TO GROWN ON

I am a big Jacksonville Jaguars fan. It's been a struggle over the years to be a fan, but I am one nonetheless. When I was evaluating season tickets in the Club section, the first number I saw for pricing was in the West Club. Let's just say those seats were $8,000 for two for the season. That number was too expensive. Then our rep shared that there was an option in the East Club with similar proximity to the field and at a similar yard line—all at a cost of just $4,000 for the season. (The cost difference has to do with the exposure to the sun and how hot it can get on the East side in early season games.) Suddenly, I was excited. All I'd have to do was deal with some heat. These seats, in my mind, were more valuable relative to the cost, since I initially had $8,000 in mind. On top of that, the rep discussed a payment plan with me that would allow us to become Club seat ticket holders for around $500 per month. There is psychology at play here. With my new $4,000 seats, I was now thinking of paying $500 monthly compared to the initial $8,000 upfront. This is seemingly much more manageable, and so we signed up!

Rule #3: Make and Gain Commitments

At some point in the process, the prospect moves from having interest in your product or service to making a commitment. This works out well if it is a two-way street. In other words, you make a commitment to the prospect before asking them to make their commitment. This creates another psychological phenomenon that sociologist Alvin Gouldner called the "norm of reciprocity." When you commit to someone, they feel naturally inclined to make a commitment back.

When working with buyers in real estate, I always looked to them for a commitment. I wanted to know that they would use my services and mine alone. No talking to other Realtors®! (Of course, I'd tell them this in far more professional wording.) I'd even have them sign something that basically said they would work with me to find their home. Not all agents do this, and sometimes there would be a little pushback. But what I found was, if I took the time first to commit to them, I had a much better chance of securing their commitment to me. I created a buyer pledge, which discussed steps of the process and what I would do for them to help them find their dream home. I would then sign this document and give it to them before I asked them to sign my buyer-broker agreement. This created a two-way commitment and made the buyers more comfortable signing with me.

Rule #4: Set Additional Expectations and Deliver Plus One

Once you have earned a commitment, lay out the next steps in the experience. This part of the process is crucial. Tell them what to expect from the product. How to best use it. How to care for it. How to get help for it. How to return it. And if you offer a service, answer questions like: What does the communication plan look like? How often will the client hear from you? How will you resolve potential conflicts?

Then—and this advice is worth gold—deliver a little more than what is expected.

I call this "Plus One" thinking. Deliver a little more in terms of support, or service, or a product feature. If you master this, you will have clients for life. And that is so tremendously valuable compared to the acquisition cost of finding new clients to replace dissatisfied ones. What you do after the sale to stay in touch really matters. Here's an example.

ONE TO GROWN ON

Have you ever dealt with a representative of a company over the phone while you are trying to get a problem resolved? Ever had to speak to two or three different representatives to solve that issue? Of course you have. We all have. If it has happened to you recently, you're probably getting irritated just now thinking about it. Sorry about that!

I was the third representative in this story back when I was in the investment field. The call came in from Jimmy, who was angry about a mutual fund that was purchased in his account. He claimed it was the wrong fund and wanted it corrected. He had spoken to two other reps over the course of a week, and both had assured him they would research the matter and call back. But neither had.

Now, the right thing to do, clearly, was research the matter and get back to him when I had an answer. And that's what I did. I knew that it would take some time to get the answer and make the change, and that we would have to pull the audio recording from the initial conversation to make sure it was us that had made the mistake. Then we would have to "bust" the trade and make the proper purchase as of the intended date. I added a "Plus One" though, and it completely saved the relationship and shifted his demeanor toward our company. It cost zero dollars and about 30 seconds. I called him back immediately after we hung up and said, "Sir, I just wanted to assure you we know how to call people back here. My name is Kevin, and my direct line is ###-####. You won't need it, but I thought that might make you a little more comfortable."

He fell all over himself thanking me for this ridiculously small and simple act. It makes sense when you think about it. Just look at it from his perspective. When we'd first hung up the phone, he had no reason to believe I would get back to him. Why would he? But now he did.

That is the magic of "Plus One" thinking. Go a little farther than what is expected.

To grow in your influence:

1. Identify the most important skill(s) you need to develop to become the best at what you do (or what you want to do).
2. Put in the research and practice to hone your craft to become the absolute best. This takes time.
3. Take action every day to put what you've learned into practice. Document the lessons learned along the way.
4. Seek out mentors—people who do something really well and who have good values. Talk to them about their journey and what it took to become the best.

When I discussed our Morning Kickstart in an earlier chapter, I mentioned the negative impact that wrong inputs—i.e., constant negativity via news outlets or worthless gossip shows—can have on your life. But the great news is that good impacts can have an equally *beneficial* positive impact! For instance, the first business book I ever read was given to me by my dad. It was about Warren Buffett, called *Buffett: The Making of an American Capitalist*. Reading that book led me to seek out credibility and work for Scott Fetzer Company, a subsidiary of Buffett's Berkshire Hathaway, selling those Kirby vacuum cleaners. This experience gave me one of the best crash courses in sales, including what to do and what not to do, which in turn led me to a sales career in mortgages, finance, and then real estate. My

ONE TO GROWN ON

level of expertise grew, and eventually I moved into a leadership role, landing a job right in my hometown of Stuart. The success in building that business led me back to Jacksonville, where I joined the executive suite at Berkshire Hathaway HomeServices Florida Network Realty. And who owns them? You guessed it! Warren Buffett!

The point:

1. Sales is influence through education. Use your sales skills ethically and always for good.
2. If you can succeed in sales, you will put yourself in a great position to transition to leadership. Leadership is influence through coaching and mentorship.
3. Aim to be great at whatever you do. Develop your skills to the point where you feel you're at the top of your game.

Three more to explore:

Power Questions by Andrew Sobel and Jerold Panas
The Little Red Book of Selling by Jeffrey Gitomer
Raving Fans by Ken Blanchard and Sheldon Bowles

KEVIN M. WAUGAMAN

Our Most Recent Blog

CHALLENGES AND SOLUTIONS

DEVELOP A CALMNESS TO YOUR STYLE

A method that works better than "Calm down!"

There is a time and place to go big. To think: Get after it! Get hyped! Get out there and make things happen for yourself! Be competitive! Aim to WIN!

But there are also times in life when a calmness to your style and approach will serve you very well.

Have you ever heard the phrase "Be the calm in the storm?" This is a really hard thing to accomplish sometimes. But it may be some of the best advice I've ever received. Being the calm in the storm has helped me navigate major challenges both personally and professionally. Let's start with an example of how being calm in the storm has helped in my personal life.

Years ago, we were in DC for a friend's wedding. We were just wrapping up the rehearsal dinner celebration the night before the big day, and Jessica (who was not yet my wife) and I were hitching a ride with a bridesmaid back to our hotel with a group from Alexandria to the Key Bridge Marriott. This bridesmaid assured us she knew her way around.

If you have ever gotten lost in the wrong part of town, you know this feeling. The next thing you know, you look around and feel as if you are in a different world. You're not even sure how you got there or how to get out. This is not a commentary on race nor an insult to the economically challenged—after all, God knows I have been there. It was, however, a group of us dressed in khakis and sportscoats driving around in what was described as "one of the most dangerous areas in our country."

The situation was made worse by the fact that Jessica had a full bladder and had to go to the bathroom. So, we stopped at a gas station. I ran inside to assess the bathroom situation and was told, "Our bathrooms aren't in use. Never are at night around here." Great. So I sprinted across the street to the other gas station. Pulling out of the station was a police officer, who asked, "What are *you* doing here?!" When I asked him to elaborate, he said, "I've got a call to attend to—but trust me, you need to get out of here!" The other gas station was the same. Their bathrooms were not in use at night.

Remember in the High C's chapter, I mentioned that one of my mentors once taught me a valuable lesson: When things around you seem to be moving fast and there is panic, slow down. Take a deep breath. Don't react or allow others to place unnecessary stress on the situation as you evaluate options. As I took a deep breath and assessed the situation, the others in the car were clearly getting frantic. The GPS wasn't working, and the gas station attendants had no interest in helping us get out of the area. There were plenty of people milling around, starting to take an interest in us.

ONE TO GROWN ON

Suddenly, I saw a tour bus turn down an alley beside the gas station. Idea! I sprinted after it. After about 100 yards, I caught up to it (it was going pretty slow). To the bus driver's surprise, I started banging on the window. It was an empty bus. He stopped, and I said, "Sir, I have a strange question for you. Do you have a bathroom on board?"

Once Jessica was relieved, our group's stress level went down a ton. We thanked the bus driver, and I started exiting the bus. But then I had another idea. I turned around and said, "Any chance you can lead us back to the Key Bridge Marriott? We're lost and would really appreciate it."

Guess what? People are good. The bus driver turned back around and led our two cars on the 20-minute ride to the Marriott. As we drove by and waved thanks, I dug into my pockets and handed him a $20 from my rolled-down window. He hadn't asked for money, but I wanted to thank him and give him some gas money for the ride. Plus, the value he provided our group in the form of a bathroom and directions far exceeded $20.

The point: Had I been frantic like the others, the situation could've been far worse.

There are also many examples that illustrate how being the calm in the storm has helped me in business. For instance, let's talk about running a business at the onset of the COVID-19 pandemic.

We had just arrived back from a real estate convention in Nashville in March 2020 when the discussion around COVID reached another level. Panic was starting to set in, and there were rumors that President Trump was getting ready to issue a national stay-at-home mandate. At the time, I held a VP role on the executive team at Berkshire Hathaway HomeServices Florida Network Realty.

A few of us needed to step up, as our CEO was out of the country and two other VPs were on vacation.

Now, I need to discuss the culture of the organization here first. One of the things our company always gets right is preparation. A couple months prior, when word was just getting out about COVID, I instructed our Operations Manager and IT Manager to start running what-if scenarios and tests. Why? To see how we would need to operate in a different environment. What equipment would we need? What security measures would we need to add if people had to work from home? How would we manage communications? How would we work with our agents and get them the information they needed. How would we train the new agents? Starting this conversation well in advance helped us move quickly when we needed to.

When things started looking serious, we expanded our small group and created our Business Continuity team. The company's founder, Linda Sherrer, was an integral part of this team and provided excellent counsel and wisdom. We outlined our initial brainstorm and started creating a phase plan and a communication plan for our employees and agents. Next, we started sending people home to work remotely before the government instituted their mandate. The team was poised, focused, and worked hard to get all our employees up and running from home. We shifted a Mega Open House weekend to a virtual event in a matter of days, started weekly company-wide webinars to maintain information flow and education, created a "steps to digital mastery" program for agents who weren't yet accustomed to the available tools, and struck the right balance of optimism and reality. None of this would have been possible if we were constantly emotional and panicky.

That said, while most of the time it is important to be the calm in the storm, it is also important to experience emotions and not totally numb yourself. Life is about managing emotions, not eliminating them. It's about creating good, safe outlets to express your emotions, not ignoring them. We are all humans, and we cannot perform authentically if we are completely devoid of emotion.

> "Life is about managing emotions, not eliminating them. It's about creating good, safe outlets to express your emotions, not ignoring them."

Sometimes it is hard to be the calm in the storm. Really hard. There was a real estate agent in South Florida who was notorious for having a terrible attitude and being downright mean. Once, she was recruited to a company and half the agents threatened to quit if the company didn't reverse her offer. It is entirely possible she had some sort of chemical imbalance, which perhaps manifested in ways that turned many people off.

Anyway, I was working with some buyers who happened to land on her listing as one they wanted to purchase. Now, real estate agents out there know that *the people* can make or break a transaction, and a professional relationship with the cooperating agent can be crucial. Sometimes, agents can get emotional and blow things up despite themselves. And in this case, this agent—let's call her Angela—was both the listing agent on the home and *the owner*.

Great. Highly volatile person + personal residence = emotions that are off the charts.

This transaction seriously tested the resolve of my "calm in the storm" approach. It was not fun. I remember sitting in her home office one time as we tried to come to terms on the post-inspection negotiations. She was screaming at me, which wasn't unusual. In fact, I may have been one of the only agents willing to meet with her in person. Many refused, instead resorting to emails and texts. As I had done with her in the past, I excused myself from the conversation and politely suggested we revisit things in a more constructive setting. We then continued the negotiations over the next couple days with the same cycle of her going nuts and me being polite.

At one point, I decided enough was enough. Even though my clients were winning in most of the areas they cared about, I was still getting quite frustrated by Angela's approach. So, I decided the only way this person might receive *my message*—that it wasn't okay to communicate with me in such a furious manner—was to give her a dose of her own medicine. I decided that the next time she snapped at me, I would raise the tone of my voice to match hers. Of course, I planned to still avoid being disrespectful or hurtful.

And you know what? It worked. We promote what we tolerate, and I needed to be clear her behavior would no longer be tolerated. The next time she got loud with me, I got loud right back. It seemed to stun her for a few moments, and she let it sink in. And then she never raised her voice at me again. This was one of the only times in my professional career that I raised my voice at someone. It shows that if someone is continuing to disrespect you and nothing else seems to work, you might have to meet them on their level. (In some cases, you should just terminate the relationship instead. You'll have to make that call.)

ONE TO GROWN ON

To enhance your calm:

1. Think of a time when you were under intense pressure.
2. Write down how you handled the situation, what you did exceptionally well, and what you could improve upon.
3. Learn from the lesson and move on. If the situation is something you regret, understand that failures and mistakes lead to growth and wisdom. The act of writing it down can often help us learn and let go.

As I brought this chapter to a close, I worked out an acronym that may help you remain calm in the face of adversity. It is an overview of my internal process:

C.A.L.M.
Collect yourself, your thoughts, and other inputs.
Assess your options. Focus on what you can control.
Lay out the path forward and communicate with others if appropriate.
Move! Or decide not to. Sometimes, doing nothing is the right answer.

When Elliott was three months old, we needed to evacuate our home in Florida for the approaching Hurricane Irma. We loaded up our luggage and got into the car to go visit my grandmother—I called her Nanny, may she rest in peace—in Brevard, North Carolina.

The trip up was pretty uneventful. We left at 3:30 a.m. to avoid traffic, though many others were leaving as well. And it wasn't too bad.

It was the return trip that left its mark.

The storm moved through Florida and eventually all the way up through North Carolina, where we were staying. It was a minor storm by then, but the winds were strong enough to knock over a bunch of trees in the mountains.

We left the day after Irma had moved through, and it seemed as if hundreds of thousands of others decide to leave at precisely the same time to head back to Florida. Trees and power lines were down all over the place. I'll never forget rounding a corner coming down out of the mountains and coming face to face with my biggest fear at the time: A car was stopped in front of us with a tree smashed into its hood.

I approached the car on foot to see if I could help, but there was no one in it. The occupants must have left and walked to get help. We found another route and kept on going.

Once we got on the highway, it was a slow crawl most of the way. The trip home, which normally takes eight hours, ended up taking double that amount. And remember how we had a three-month-old with us? Amazing as he is and was, there was plenty of screaming, diaper changing, and drama. I stopped for gas often since we were told it was scarce all across the Eastern Seaboard.

Once we reached Georgia, we were thrilled to find our generous neighbors to the north had shut down all exits to everyone except residents. In other words, there were no more options for gas, and we were now changing our son's diapers on the side of Interstate 95 (by we, I mean Jessica—she was a real champ). Had I not had a calmness to my style, I would have been totally stressed out. Will we find gas? How can we get E to stop crying? Is this the fastest way? Why is Waze not working? Every once in a while, the traffic would clear a bit and some people would start flying around, driving like maniacs. What was wrong with these people?

The feelings of anger and stress were there. I was angry at the flying cars, angry at the politicians in Georgia, and angry at myself for not leaving at 3:30 a.m. like we had on the way up.

I frequently took deep breaths, and we tried to play some games along the way to get E laughing as often as possible. I am sure divorces were happening all over Interstate 95 that day. Also, I reminded myself that when I was 16, I would have been one of the idiots driving like a maniac in a naive attempt to get home faster. I'm pretty sure I even spotted a vision of my former self in my 1991 240SX whizzing by us at one point.

Sometimes you don't have 16 hours to work on and exhibit your calmness. Sometimes you need to make a snap decision without panic. This is precisely why it is so important to cultivate a calmness over time. That way, when you need it in a snap, it's already there.

Here's another driving story (because the road is a great place to practice your calmness). We were driving back to Jacksonville from South Florida after visiting family. My dad taught me years ago that when driving it is important to spend a percentage of the time glancing in the rearview and side mirrors to know what is behind and beside you. Thankfully, I now do this non-consciously when driving. So, traveling 70 mph, I thankfully had a calmness to my style and an awareness of my surroundings when the car in front of me darted to the right to avoid a weed wacker in the middle of our center lane. In less than a second, without panicking, I knew what I had to do: slam into the weed wacker head on.

You see, without looking, I already knew there were cars approaching at higher speeds in the lanes on both sides of me. A move into a different lane would have caused a major accident. I also knew there was a car directly behind me, so slamming on the brakes wasn't an option. The best action was to hit the wacker head on, accept the damage, and then look for an opportunity to get off the road.

And that's exactly what we did. The choice blew out a tire and dented one of our rims. Still, that was better than having someone slam into us at high speeds—or worse, cause us to spin out and flip over. If I was not calm, the situation could have been disastrous.

The point:

1. Emotions happen. Address them, talk about them, and establish methods to manage your stress. Then, take action. And don't wallow in a victim mentality.
2. This is where a solid mindset and Morning Kickstart pay off. Slow down, take deep breaths, and remember to focus on steps you can take each day to accomplish what is needed. Limit or eliminate any time spent thinking about what you cannot control.
3. Be sensitive to others. We are all doing the best we can based on our upbringing and our beliefs. Don't assume everyone has read a book like this and has the tools to perform under pressure.

ONE TO GROWN ON

We promote what we tolerate. If someone is being disrespectful, it's okay to stand up for yourself—even if it doesn't feel like the "calm in the storm" thing to do.

Three more to explore:

How to Stop Worrying and Start Living by Dale Carnegie
The Power of Intention by Dr. Wayne Dyer
You Can Heal Your Life by Louise L. Hay

Our Most Recent Blog

OPPORTUNITY COST AND THE CREDIT CARD CRISIS

Caution! Keep away! Do not enter! Danger!

I needed some credit! It was the early 2000s, and I was taking my girlfriend at the time on a short vacation to San Antonio. The problem? I didn't have any money. Or, to put things more accurately, I didn't have the amount of money I thought I needed to impress this young woman on our vacation. I had done the research, and the waterfront hotel I wished to stay at was three times more expensive than staying at a Holiday Inn and 10 times more than staying at a Motel 6.

I also made reservations at only the finest restaurants—there would be no Applebee's on this little trip. Fast food? Heck no. Only the finest.

The trip was a blast, though she and I broke up not long afterwards. Meanwhile, I was still paying for the trip many years later. In fact, I was still paying for the trip after she'd married a different dude! Now, to her credit (pun intended), she had always been willing to contribute. She picked up meals and even one of the hotel rooms. But that's not the point. We'll get to the point soon enough.

If you have lots of credit card debt and feel overwhelmed, stop the bleeding now. Put the cards down. If you are just like I was in my late teens—just starting to let loose with debt—put it down!

Financially speaking, this is a serious concept to grasp. Credit card debt and the associated interest charges have had a major financial impact on my life. It's absurd, really!

For whatever reason, I was a big spender throughout my late teens and early 20s. I had zero awareness of what the debt would do to me financially over the years if left undealt with. My father had tried to warn me, but for some reason his advice didn't stick. My biggest spends were on alcohol and partying. I was always willing to pick up a tab, to buy someone dinner, to supply parties with food and wine. I was so generous—and so poor. And I was making my future self even poorer.

Instant gratification is a tough opponent. It worked against me in other areas too. You mean I can have that nice suit now and only pay a few dollars per month to own it? Sign me up!

But you know what? It adds up. It adds up big time.

Want to know a secret? I was paying for the credit card debt I racked up in my 20s well into my 40s. Sure, it was restructured a bit and rolled over and moved back and forth to a zero-interest option. And my dad even stepped in at one point to consolidate everything at a reasonable interest rate compared to the credit card gouging. In my mid-20s, I even made some progress and almost had it all paid off. But then I brilliantly started a real estate career right before the Great Recession. No surprise, I plunged back into debt during my first two years in real estate. That meant my wife and children (who had nothing to do with my debt) paid for it as well during those years. How? Because we lost out on all the investments we could've made over the years. It was an enormously expensive learning lesson. Sorry, dear. Sorry, kids.

Let's talk about opportunity cost for a minute. Opportunity cost means that every dollar I spend—if not spent optimally—has a cost associated with it regarding what that money could have done elsewhere. For example, holding cash has an opportunity cost associated with it. If I keep $1,000 in a safe in my home, that may be okay as an emergency fund. But if I could make an investment with that $1,000 that could earn me a 10% return over a year, the opportunity cost of what I chose to do with that money is $100 per year. That's not great!

This is important stuff! Don't move on until you grasp this idea.

The following is an extreme example. I know most of us need transportation, but let us look at the true cost of a car (excluding tax, tag title, and other fees). Let's say you buy a car for $30,000 with 10% down and at 5% interest over five years. That car costs you $3,000 down plus five years of amortized payments at $510 per month—just over $30,000 in payment over five years. The total cost of that car is $33,600 and change before even considering maintenance, gas, insurance, etc.

Now, let's say instead you take that $3,000 and invest it at 5% interest over five years, and then add that $510 per month into the investment instead of to the vehicle. Instead of a declining asset (assets that tend to lose value over time) that costs you $33,000 over five years, you would have acquired $38,000 and change. That's a net worth swing of up to nearly $71,000 over five years! Some of the ride sharing options or lower priced cars might seem a little more palatable, at least early in the wealth-building process.

Again, I know you need to get places, but maybe putting less money towards a declining asset like a car, and then putting the difference to work in an asset that is more likely to appreciate over time (real estate, stocks, funds, fixed income, etc.) is a good idea. One of the biggest financial mistakes people make early, in addition to racking up credit card debt, is buying a car they can't afford. According to Progressive, cars lose 20% of their value in the first year on average, and then up to 15% more per year until the four- or five-year mark. Unless you're a mechanic or an entrepreneur whose business is buying cheap cars, fixing them up, and successfully selling them for a profit, you ought to spend less than you want on a car. I'm not going to give you a percentage of income here as a guide, as that can be super misleading. Some people say to spend between 10-15% of your income on a car payment. But that does not ring true for someone paying too much for rent and/or their credit card debt. Look at your budget, see what you can afford while still saving at least 10% for the future, and make the right call.

Opportunity cost also applies to your time and how you spend it. Every minute you spend on something that doesn't give you a return of happiness, financial gain, or relationship building—i.e., the things that matter most—is time gone forever. When you say yes to things that don't align with who you are

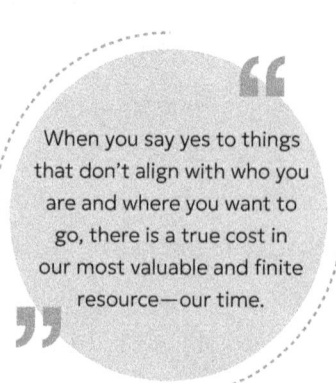

When you say yes to things that don't align with who you are and where you want to go, there is a true cost in our most valuable and finite resource—our time.

ONE TO GROWN ON

and where you want to go, there is a true cost in our most valuable and finite resource—our time.

Allow me to illustrate this in terms of a sales job. Let's say Jake sells lawn services to high-net-worth families. He gathers accounts by networking and developing relationships with luxury real estate agents in the area. He also spends time at events where those people gather. To gain referrals, Jake's best use of time involves calling his current accounts to make sure they are satisfied and offering to correct any shortcomings when he hears about them. His time is worth $200 per hour because he has a very successful practice.

Let's say one of Jake's employees calls in sick and ends up being out for a week. Instead of having any back-up solutions or going through the efforts of hiring someone, Jake decides to roll up his sleeves and jump on a mower himself. He is now doing work that is valued currently by the marketplace at closer to $20 per hour. Every single hour that Jake spends on the mower carries an opportunity cost of $200 dollars, which would net $180 in terms of real dollars. That's expensive over time!

I get it. There are many variables here. And yes, it is good every once in a while for the boss to get on the front lines to stay sharp and interact with employees and clients. No doubt, you need to evaluate that stuff. But the idea here is not to get too loose with how you choose to invest your time and money. There is more at stake. Be intentional.

Okay, that's a simplified lesson on opportunity cost. Now, back to our theme of credit card debt and how this all applies.

One opportunity cost of my debt spiral was a potential investment with a friend of mine, a very successful venture capitalist. The year was 1999, and the normal minimum investment for his fund was $1,000,000. But for a temporary period, they opened a friends and family program for anyone who could put together $10,000. Since I was servicing credit card debt to the tune of $800 per month (just in minimum payments!), I was unable to gather the funds. Now, had I made that $10,000 investment and then rolled the proceeds into each of the 32 subsequent funds, the value of that investment 20 years later would be just under $1 million!

The only use of credit cards that makes financial sense is when you pay off the balance every month. Or if there is a true emergency—like life-or-death stuff. Or if you are doing something in the personal development field and have a *legit* plan to pay it back. You know, investing in yourself. But that is IT.

Check the math here: I spend $10,000 over the course of a year and I carry the balance at 15% interest. If I'm making the minimum payments (assuming a 2% minimum), I would pay back more than $25,000 over the course of 30 years. (This what-if scenario was taken directly from a credit card statement). This wasn't something that happened all at once. It was a little here, a little there, and it all added up until I reached a point of, "How did I get here?" A few times in my life, my credit card debt felt like a noose tightening around my neck. It kept me up at night constantly. It was never worth it.

So: Earn it, save and donate some, invest some, then spend it.

To be clear, and to help you avoid this pitfall: If you add up the interest alone paid back over the years in addition to the opportunity cost, credit card debt cost me and my family over one million dollars. That is an eye opener! It all started with a $500-limit credit card I got back in college. No biggie, I thought. But then came another $500 card, which I also maxed out. Then a limit increase here, a new card there. I was hooked.

ONE TO GROWN ON

(Possible invention: A device you attach to your credit card that sends a sizable electric shock through your body every time you touch the card. Not every time you use it—every time you touch it!)

I have learned that many of life's great experiences don't need to cost a lot of money. Hiking, biking (aside from the initial cost), visiting parks, and going to the beach don't cost money. Neither does reading, gathering with friends and family, or playing many sports.

American radio personality Dave Ramsey once said, "If you will **live like no one else**, later you can **live like no one else**." Little decisions made every day add up. One dollar spent on something unnecessary versus deposited in an interest-bearing bank account turns out to be way more than one dollar over time—especially if you use a credit card and end up paying interest on those dollars,

Living responsibly today means paying attention to your budget, saving a portion of your money, and living on less than your income. It may mean you can't go to all the parties, or buy that new dress yet, or get the lobster on the menu. But if you make good decisions and strive to get your financial house in order, those things will be available to you in the future. It's about sacrifice and discipline. It has nothing to do with not living life. You can live a great and fruitful life within your means, and it will mean less stress along the way.

By the way, please don't miss the point here. We are talking about *bad* use of debt. Stuff like loading up on credit cards. Or loans to finance depreciating assets like cars and boats even though you can't afford the payments. There is good debt too, like using leverage to finance appreciating assets or create businesses. If you are going to use debt, focus on appreciating assets that generally involve some combination of the following:

- Scarcity: There is generally less of it available than would satisfy demand.
- Demand: People want and/or need the asset.
- Utility: It is useful.
- Value: It creates some sort of value for the owner and/or others.
- Transferability: It can be traded or sold for profit.

Some examples of assets that are more likely to appreciate over time (of course, there are no guarantees) include:

- Real estate (commercial and residential)
- Stocks (ownership of underlying businesses)
- Mutual funds
- Index funds
- Fixed income investments (bonds, bond funds, treasuries)
- Rare coins, artwork, and other collectibles

Just do your homework and don't over-leverage yourself. And don't become personally liable for debt beyond what you can handle.

On the flip side, our great strengths can also become weaknesses. It is possible to become so frugal with money that you start missing out on opportunities and become enamored with a number in your bank account that makes you feel good. In this case, the acquisition and saving of money becomes too much of a mistress. It is important to be, as John Maxwell says, "a river, not a reservoir." I would try to find a good balance between earning, spending, blessing others, and saving. None of which require going into debt with credit cards.

ONE TO GROWN ON

What do you think the next step is to avoid or reduce your debt? I bet you know the answers.

To excel financially:

1. Make a budget if you don't have one. Do it now. Earn, live, give, save, and spend what's left.
2. Stick to that budget even if you're uncomfortable for a while. Future you will be thankful and wealthier.
3. If you have debt, seek advice and counsel on consolidation or legal options. Philosophically, bankruptcy was not for me. But many reputable people have been through it. And if done properly, there is no shame in it.
4. Analyze your current expenses to identify your necessities. To get on the right path, you may need to cut out cable, streaming services, or other luxuries for a bit. You could always read instead—books from the library are free!—and then you will notice a dramatic compound effect on your time and money.
5. Look into ways to invest money with low fees. Check into Fidelity, Acorns—there are several apps out there to help you manage this. Just get started, even if it seems like you're investing trivial amounts. With small steps, investing will become a habit that significantly impacts your net worth.

George Samuel Clason, in *The Richest Man in Babylon*[1], suggests the following formula:

- 10% of your income is yours to keep (savings)

- 70% should cover your expenses (shelter, transportation, food, taxes)
- 20% should be used to pay off debts (especially high interest and non-deductible debt such as debt from credit cards)

You will need to figure out how giving fits into the equation for you. One suggestion would be to be a little more aggressive early on in paying off debt to better position yourself to help others financially. If you are constantly struggling to make ends meet, blessing others financially becomes harder.

Actor Will Rogers once said, "Too many people spend money they haven't earned, to buy things they don't want, to impress people that they don't like."

You don't need to be one of these people. If you have been heading down this path, you have choices to make to get back on the wealth-building path.

The point:

Don't spend it if you don't have it.
Put the credit card down.

Three more to explore to dive deeper on this subject:

The Richest Man in Babylon by George S. Clason
The Total Money Makeover by Dave Ramsey
Investing For Dummies by Eric Tyson and Tony Levene

ONE TO GROWN ON

Our Most Recent Blog

---

[1] George Samuel Clason, *The Richest Man in Babylon*, Penguin Books, 1926.

CHALLENGES INDICATE PROGRESS

Growth and consequences

I was sitting at the closing table for my first non-personal-property sale in real estate. I was a bit full of myself at the time. There I was kicked back in my chair, chatting with my buyer around a big mahogany table. At one point in the process, there seemed to be a bit of confusion, and I heard my name repeated a couple times. "Kevin, Kevin? Escrow?" Escrow is a term used to describe money that is held by a third party at the beginning of a real estate transaction. This money gets distributed appropriately and the escrow account is in a sense closed, hence the term "closing." In this case, my buyer had deposited the escrow funds with my brokerage. We had all showed up ready to finalize the deal, and all the money was there except for the $5,000 check I had forgotten to request from our processor and deliver. Now all eyes were on me. It was incredibly embarrassing.

Thankfully, the wise words of my company's owner Steve Bohner rang in my ears, "If you ain't got no problems, you ain't doin' no business."

The growth that leads to the biggest return in our lives generally happens when we are outside of our comfort zone. If we are going to move outside of this zone, we must make mistakes. And if you want to get better at something, you must get your mind right about the fact that humans make mistakes. When I was near the end of my time in financial services, I had a pretty good handle on things. I'd become a bit of a go-to-guy for business analysis, special projects the firm was launching, and certain technology systems. As I mentioned earlier, when I moved into real estate, I erroneously believed I needed to master everything before I did anything. So, I took every class offered by my company and the local real estate association. I took several of these classes two or three times. It was very expensive to learn all I needed to learn. But being a student was in my comfort zone. I love learning, and there is nothing wrong with that.

The growth that leads to the biggest return in our lives generally happens when we are outside of our comfort zone.

But like everything in life, excess has its downside. What do you do after you learn? You practice. Then you DO! Often, it's the practice and the doing that take us out of our comfort zones. This is where the real learning and growth happens.

Back to that story about my first closing. I had been taught during training that I needed to request an escrow check three days in advance and take it to the attorney's office. But when did I *really* learn that lesson?!

Thankfully, the attorney had worked with us before many times and closed the transaction and let me deliver the check later that afternoon. This speaks to the power of relationships and trust. I am very thankful I didn't need to delay everyone and run back to the office while they all sat twiddling their thumbs.

It took me a while to realize that discomfort is actually a good thing. It is where we build relationships with others who are in similar situations. It is where our incomes grow. It is where our spiritual journey deepens, and it is where we begin to expand our comfort zone! Early in my sales career, I feared making cold calls. Then I got comfortable taking a first step, picking up the phone, and dialing the number. When the call didn't go as planned, I would write down the objection and the lesson I learned. The real lesson was this: As long as I approached someone from a place of service, who really cared how they perceived me?

As I continue to share some of the mistakes I have made, please know that I'm not trying to keep you from making mistakes of your own. Not at all. However, by avoiding silly mistakes that have long-term impact, you can put yourself in position to make *better* mistakes.

Huh?

Let's go back to my credit card example. If I had thought through some of the choices I made spending money I didn't have—if I had perhaps lived on a budget—I may have saved money and decided to open up the restaurant/sports bar/night club concept I had dreamed about in college. Now, racking up major credit card debt was a mistake. However, had I saved the money and even borrowed some money to start the restaurant, it may have failed. Which would be the "better" mistake? I would argue that the start-up would have provided far more valuable learning for potential future ventures than overspending on hotels and parties. Let's take it one step further: I wouldn't even call starting that sports bar, even if it had failed, a mistake. It would have been a growth opportunity through and through.

That's the ticket. The mistakes we make are opportunities for reflection and growth. Without this mindset, we view mistakes as problems, and we beat ourselves up. This causes a negative feedback loop in our non-conscious brain. And then we unknowingly relive the negativity over and over again.

Mistakes are part of life. Sometimes it takes hitting rock bottom for people to make a change. If that is where you are right now, I feel for you. I've been there financially and emotionally and can promise you from personal experience that everything will be okay if you work on your attitude and start acting in a positive manner.

There are some mistakes to avoid if you can. These mistakes have major consequences over time. I'm talking about the mistakes that could potentially cause harm to others, that result from behavior you wouldn't normally engage in. I'm talking about abuse of alcohol and use of mind-altering drugs. In terms of alcohol abuse, I have experience. Thankfully, I've never hurt anyone physically, but I am quite certain I've hurt the feelings of many people along the way. Trust me, it's not worth it. I've partied so hard into the morning that I've slept away entire days. Again, it's not worth it.

I have a relative who hit and killed a pedestrian driving home one night after five beers. I know a good family man who struck his wife one night after too much to drink. Unsafe sex. Date rape. Suicide. All these things become more probable when we are out of our minds in a bad way.

One story I'll share has stayed with me ever since it happened. It is a funny story, but please know that much worse can happen.

ONE TO GROWN ON

I was with my two friends Andy and Julia, walking back to our dorm from a party one night. It was a chilly evening in Elon, and we were laughing and carrying on. Up ahead, I noticed an alcohol checkpoint. The officers were likely checking for intoxicated drivers, but the situation still made me nervous. I had the bright idea to take a left and walk around the checkpoint on a parallel road. As we charted our new path, one of us—I can't remember who the instigator was—decided it was time to urinate. So, we stepped off the road, found the nearest building and a nearby bush for Julia, and commenced. Julia was making all kinds of noise in the bushes while Andy and I were facing the wall. I turned around to shush Julia, and just as I did, I saw the flashlight appear on her. One of the officers from the checkpoint apparently had thought it would be wise to go check on the loud, obnoxious college kids who were trying to avoid the checkpoint!

I quickly zipped up. Then I stood there, frozen, as my eyes followed the flashlight beam from Julia to Andy. Andy had also zipped up, and he'd immediately started trying to convince the officer that he was just standing there waiting for Julia. But the flashlight slowly moved down to his crotch, where some unfortunate evidence remained.

While this exchange was going on, I'd decided my red flannel jacket had saved me. The wall we were urinating on was made of brick, I was about 15 feet away, and it was dark. I'd even positioned myself as flat as I could against the wall, like Jim Carrey in *Ace Ventura Pet Detective* when he breaks in to find the Dolphin. My arms and legs were sprawled out and not moving at all. As I started planning my escape, I was jolted back to reality with these memorable words: "I see you too, dumbass."

The officer was furious. So I asked him, man to man, "Why is this such a problem? Have you never taken a leak outside?" He ignored me at first. Once I was secured in the back of his police cruiser, he glared at me in the rearview and said, in a beautiful North Carolina accent, "Boy, next time you need to relieve yourself, I'd appreciate it if you didn't do it on my church."

Yikes. So *that* was the building we chose?! Oops.

I wish I could say the story ended there. The tickets we were given didn't have any dollar amount or court date on them, so we assumed—yes, assumed—that we'd gotten off with warnings. About two months later, while I was in class one evening, a roommate of mine appeared at the door waving his arms, trying to get my attention. It was so dramatic that I thought maybe something bad had happened to someone I cared about. I excused myself and joined him outside the classroom. He told me the police were at my dorm room and had a warrant for my arrest.

"What?!"

Something bad *was* happening. To both Andy and me. It turned out we were supposed to either pay a fine or appear in court, but we'd failed to do so. Failure to appear in court is a misdemeanor, which carried with it another series of fines—and a charge on my record. All because of public urination! Every time I get a professional license now or join a new company, because I am someone who believes in full disclosure, I feel the need to tell this story. Thankfully, the story is usually met with laughter, and I still get hired. Even the judge who granted us our nolo contendere request was laughing as he brought his gavel down.

ONE TO GROWN ON

Have you ever heard that phrase "nothing good happens after midnight?" Well, it's not totally true, but it is true that you need to be more careful after midnight!

To take better risks:

1. Think about the habits in your life that make you more prone to bad mistakes.
2. Reduce or eliminate those habits from your life.
3. If you go through days feeling a high level of comfort, you should probably be taking more calculated risks. Think about something that is a bit of a risk but that would help you develop personally or professionally. Take the first action step toward doing that thing.

When I am out and about nowadays, and especially when it comes to work gatherings, I typically arrive back home or back at the hotel (if I am traveling) no later than 9:30 p.m. At work functions, I leave when the drinks really start flowing. This irritates people sometimes, as many would prefer me to stay out and socialize. But that doesn't matter to me. Because the chance you'll end up involved in conflict and/or a misunderstanding goes up dramatically the later you stay out. And that's true whether you are drinking or not!

For years now, personal growth has been part of my proactive life plan. The key is to learn and then take action. That's why this book is filled with examples of proactive steps to take. When you mess up, learn from it, and then move on. Don't ruminate on the matter. If you replay the mistake over and over in your head, you'll do a number on your non-conscious brain. Trust me, I've been there.

If replaying mistakes over and over is a problem for you, here is a strategy. Start a journal and write down at least one win you have each day—even the minor wins. Then, when you make a mistake, write down what happened, what you could do better next time, and the main learning lesson!

The point:

1. Most mistakes are good and lead to tremendous growth.
2. A lot of significant growth happens outside of your comfort zone.
3. Avoid putting yourself in positions where bad mistakes are more likely.

Three more to explore:

Sometimes You Win Sometimes You Learn by John Maxwell
Make the Impossible Possible by Bill Strickland
The Energy Bus by Jon Gordon

ONE TO GROWN ON

Our Most Recent Blog

YOUR INCOME IS EQUAL TO YOUR ABILITY TO SOLVE PROBLEMS

Converting problems to opportunities

Who likes problems? I do. Because these days I recognize that problems are actually opportunities.

Yes, opportunities. Let's reframe the problem into a challenge. After all, we all love a good challenge. Challenges lead to opportunities. They always have and they always will. Step up to the challenge!

In the last chapter, we identified that challenges indicate progress. Now we will break challenges down even further to offer strategic ideas on how to overcome them. Reframe your problems into challenges, and your challenges into opportunities.

The bicycle was born from an 1815 invention called the running machine, which was built to replace horses as a more efficient way to get around. The printing press, refrigerator, ambulance, and computer were all born from various pandemics, wars, and other crises over the years.

Anyone can function in optimal circumstances. But what value can a person bring if everything always runs smoothly? In fact, if everything always ran smoothly, working human beings would become commodities. And in that instance, what would stop the automation of everything?

Thankfully, we live in an imperfect world consisting of imperfect people. There are always challenges and opportunities out there. Solving problems has a direct impact on your ability to earn a wage, and the greater your ability to solve problems, the greater your capacity to earn!

I see five main sources of challenges in today's world:

1. Communication
2. Drama
3. Inefficient systems
4. A need or desire for change
5. Expectation vs. reality gap

#1 and #5 are by far mankind's greatest sources of confusion, problems, ill will, negotiation failure, and mistrust. So, we will begin and end with these.

Let's start with this statement: Poor communication is the core of most of our challenges.

I like to say that better communication solves most everything.

There are two barriers to communication. The first is that communication takes time. It requires an investment, and often it must be in the form of getting face to face or voice to voice with someone. Many people simply avoid proper communication because they think they don't have time for it.

The other barrier to pure communication is that we are humans and emotional creatures! What I am communicating to you can easily be misunderstood based on your view of the world, and so can any potential emotions I am creating in you as I deliver the message. Even with my wife, I sometimes watch her reaction as I am speaking, and I think, "Why is she getting mad? I'm complimenting her!"

One of the departments that reported to me during my real estate leadership career was IT. We had a recurring problem at one of our offices—the Wi-Fi kept shutting down and kicking agents off the network. Two issues emerged during the solution phase of this challenge.

When the issue was brought to my attention, it had already existed for a period of time. So, that was a communication issue in and of itself. There were two agents in particular whose lack of communication needed to be addressed. To coordinate the resolution, these agents would need to be on site at the same time to work through the issue with a third-party vendor. If you know anything about real estate agents, you know that the productive ones are on the move all the time. They are not posted up at an office all day. This third-party vendor, I was told, was facing a major delay in delivering support. We were told that when we submitted a ticket, they would get back to us within a week.

And here's the rub: Once they responded, the agents would have *fifteen minutes'* notice to get to the office and receive the tech support call. Simply put, it was ludicrous.

My IT manager was frustrated as well. He assured me this was the protocol and there was nothing to be done about it. He had discussed it with his contact at the company and was told we would just have to make do with it. Hopefully when the call came in, the agents would be available.

Well, on my commute home one day, I decided to try something. Before leaving, and instead of calling our contact at the company, I looked up the main 800 number for this vendor on Google and called it. A sales rep answered. "May I explain something to you?" I asked. "I am an existing client and I'd like to talk something through."

The call lasted all of fifteen minutes—my entire commute. By the end of it—and I was mainly asking questions and listening—we had reached our resolution. It was so simple. We would wait for the response to our ticket and then schedule a support window where both agents could coordinate and get to the office at a designated time. We'd combined our two solutions, and it all made perfect sense to me. It may have taken an extra day versus what we would have liked, but it didn't put an unreasonable stress on us, the client. It's just a shame it took so many phone calls and emails to reach the level of communication needed to solve the problem.

Another issue we were dealing with around the same time had to do with external interference to our Wi-Fi. Our tech team ran test after test—resetting things, changing passwords—and concluded that an external component was causing the problem. They provided a handful of solutions, and there was even a concern about potential malicious intent. I asked, "Has anyone gone to the businesses on either side of us and asked if they've been having any issues with their system? Perhaps they inadvertently set something up recently that is now interfering with our Wi-Fi?"

It turned out the neighbor to the north of the office had just had a tech company set up their Wi-Fi, and guess what? They had errantly placed a setting on their system that negatively impacted ours. Need to solve a problem? Get face to face when possible. We wasted hours of time behind a computer trying to figure this out. All the systems tests and checks could not answer the question.

As a broker and leader of a real estate company with many years' worth of experience, I often get called in when complex negotiations are going sideways, or when an agent has trouble communicating with a separate party regarding a transaction. After lots of listening and question asking, I generally ask the agent what they think the problem is. In many cases, they respond, "The other side just doesn't get it. I need you to get involved."

"Okay. Let's talk about communication," I say. "Talk to me about what was said and how it was said."

They usually say, "He said this, she said that, I said this, etc.," for a few minutes.

"Okay, great. And how did you communicate?"

Blank stare.

"What was the means of communication?"

If there was a communication gap, I already knew the answer.

"Emails and text messages."

"Okay. You know I am always happy and ready to jump in the pool and help. The only prerequisite I have is that you attempt to resolve this matter in a face-to-face environment first. Drive across town, meet the other agent for coffee, and try to hash this out in person." If the other person was out of town, I'd recommend a voice call or video chat instead. In some cases, if the matter was important enough, I would recommend getting on a plane to speak face to face.

I would help the agent strategize an approach, which usually meant ensuring the other side felt heard and understood.

I've had this conversation dozens of times over the years, and 95% of the time the problem would get resolved without me getting in the middle. Best of all, I've helped someone become a better communicator and negotiator instead of doing the work for them.

Relationships are so important. When you have solid relationships in place, the communication piece is so much easier. If you don't have good relationships, I would encourage you to spend some time building connection with and getting to know the people you're often placed in challenging situations with. Then take the time to really try to understand their point of view.

Strengthening relationships and adding to your network will make problem solving so much easier. You will be able to add tremendous value to others' lives along the way, and they in turn will be there for you.

To become a better problem solver:

1. Set a goal to strengthen your current relationships. Write on your calendar: "I will call or get together with one person each week to further develop the relationship."
2. Expand your network. Write on your calendar: "I will add one more relationship to my network each week or month by attending events or tapping into my community."
3. Here is an easy one: Ask more questions as you attempt to solve problems.

ONE TO GROWN ON

Stephen Covey said, "Seek first to understand, then to be understood." This is critical in all aspects of life both personally and professionally. I would add another layer to his saying: Seek first to understand, **communicate your understanding**, then to be understood. How do we communicate our understanding? It all starts with asking questions and listening. Then you must repeat back what you think you heard the other person say and ask if you got it right. Pretty simple, huh? Next, you can find points of agreement before making your point.

Next on our list is the drama challenge. This has to do with emotions getting out of control. Some people are brought up surrounded by constant drama, and so it becomes their way of operating. That's okay, but it doesn't mean you need to operate on their level. Don't judge. Drama frequently creates challenges and negative emotions. Your job in overcoming challenges is to minimize anything that would add to the drama and instead work to neutralize it.

Similar to improving our communication, one way to improve dramatic situations or relationships is to express empathy for the other person. Say something like, "I can see this is clearly influencing you in a bad way. I hope we can clear things up so we can be productive in our time together. Is there anything else you think we need to address before getting started?" This will be far more effective than saying, "You need to calm down. We aren't getting anywhere."

Dramatic people don't necessarily think they are being dramatic. In fact, they might think *you're* the dramatic one. And sometimes they are right. If you are making decisions and speaking straight from your emotions and things seem difficult, it may be time to breathe and step back to ask yourself a few questions:

1. How am I feeling?
2. Do I understand the other person's perspective?
3. Will I feel good about how I am acting tomorrow, after the dust settles?
4. Will this issue matter to me one year from now?

If you are angry or sad, it may be better to step back from the challenge. Once you have, frame the matter to focus on working together to solve the problem. It's not always easy, but the rewards and the relationships earned will be far greater than the short-term wins you might be gunning for.

Another challenge creator is an inefficient system or way of conducting business. If you are going to be effective at any task, you must have processes in place. Sometimes, it is important to review and update these processes, especially when you consider that technology and ways of doing things are always evolving. For instance, when was the last time you broke down a process in your life, your Morning Kickstart, what you do when you get to work, how you put together that presentation, how you manufacture that widget, or how you delegate certain functions?

Chances are there are some processes in your life you could stand to improve. It may be as simple as moving your workout clothes to a different area in your closet so things are more organized. Maybe it's moving all your Morning Kickstart reading and writing materials closer to your chair. Perhaps it's organizing your work area so your key materials are within reach. Or maybe your smartphone apps can be better organized, allowing you to find them easier.

Or it might be something in your work processes. Let's start with basics. If there is something you do in your work that is frequently repeated, have a look at the process and see if it can be improved. Write down the steps of the process so it is something you can duplicate and measure. The chapter "Ideas Are Cheap, Execution is Gold" details my work in developing a real estate business development process.

One other example of how we improve work processes is how we created a process around webinar meetings. When COVID-19 first hit and we moved toward the virtual arena, meetings required a lot of time and effort. Once we realized these types of meetings weren't going away, we looked at the process and put it down in writing:

1. Decide the topic and guest speakers one month in advance.
2. Start a DRAFT of the slide deck from our template.
3. Set the webinar up and generate the link.
4. Invite all the panelists and send out the form email we created with all instructions.
5. Market the webinar beginning two weeks in advance.
6. Monitor registration numbers and share them with the leadership team.
7. Finalize the slides.
8. A/V check meeting day before.
9. Final A/V check 15 minutes before meeting.
10. Conduct the meeting.

This process ensured we were well prepared for every meeting and that the A/V issues you often hear about were kept to a minimum. It still works well for virtual meetings.

The need or desire for change can create challenges. Some change is good, while some is not. All change, though, can create the opportunity to overcome challenges and get better or do better. Many people are fearful of change. I recommend finding a way to embrace it and get more comfortable with it. The only thing constant in this world is change—and one of the only reasons to fight change is if it somehow violates one of your principles.

All change can create the opportunity to overcome challenges and get better or do better.

Finally, we arrive at our last challenge/opportunity: missed expectations. Some of the biggest disappointments and conflicts occur when expectations are set and not met. Be very careful in this regard! The gap between expectations and reality can erode trust and put a lid on your potential earnings.

As I've said, we are all in sales to some extent in our lives. One thing we make clear when we are training salespeople is that expectation setting can make or break a career. So, try setting realistic expectations, and then look for some "Plus Ones" to exceed those expectations. Deliver on what you say you are going to do and be honest about the product you are delivering. That way, your expectations should align with reality.

Think about a time when you got really upset. I am guessing there was a component of either miscommunication or missed expectations. See why setting reasonable expectations is so important?

Here's another story. A group of friends and I were out early one morning during our high school senior cruise—somewhere in

ONE TO GROWN ON

Nassau in the Bahamas. Around 10 of us had split off from the group to go find some jet skis and fly around the bay on crystal clear water. Since a few of us didn't have much money, we paired up. My good friend Travis was the first one to try and drive with me on the back. He was terrible (although in hindsight, maybe I should have let him try a bit more). We switched places, and then I got us up and running. We were having a blast ... for about five minutes. (Or maybe it was only two minutes. Honestly, it's all a bit hazy now.)

What I do remember was that we were all going about as fast as we could. I noticed one of our friends had taken an interesting angle coming towards us from the right side. I kept going, and to my surprise, so did our friend. He was trying to jump our wake, I was later told. But I didn't realize that at the time. (Also, if you know anything about jet skis, you know "jumping a wake" is a silly idea.)

Well, as he came barreling down on us, I panicked and turned my jet ski away. That slowed us down, but it was too late. A huge collision shattered both jet skis. Travis had seen it coming, and thank God, he slid off the back and got himself under water before impact. Our friend went flying through the air and skipped across the water. Meanwhile, I took the full brunt of impact and was unconscious for the next hour. When I finally awoke, I watched as the Carnival Cruise Line surgeon stitched a ligament in my arm back together. It could have been so much worse. Thankfully, a stitched-up arm and serious neck pain for about a month was all I suffered. This is a scary example of expectations versus reality. My friend had expected us to keep going straight at full speed, and I had expected my friend not to drive like an asshole! Reality? We collided!

Let's recap:

1. Communication – Do this well, and you will create long-lasting and mutually beneficial relationships. Do it poorly, and life will be a struggle.
2. Drama – Keep it to a minimum. You know, don't throw unnecessary fuel on an already ripping-hot fire.
3. Inefficient systems – Seek consistent improvement so you are equipped to help people move from point A to point B.
4. Need or desire for change – Ask questions and listen. That way, you will fully understand someone's objective.
5. Expectation vs. reality gap – Do what you say you will do! Apologize if you are unable to deliver. And don't make excuses.

As you get more intentional about recognizing these sources of challenges, you will be better prepared to work through them, grow, and evolve. And you will be better positioned to increase your potential earnings as a result.

The point:

1. If something doesn't make sense, question it. And keep after a better solution in the meantime.
2. Get face to face or voice to voice with people to overcome challenges.
3. Always try to put relationships first. The better you are at this, the stronger your ability to overcome challenges and grow.

ONE TO GROWN ON

Please don't shy away from challenges. Challenges are leading indicators of momentum in both business and life. If you don't have challenges, or your challenges seem small, chances are you're living life small.

Three more to explore:

How to Win Friends and Influence People by Dale Carnegie
Rainmaking Conversations by Mike Schultz and John E. Doerr
The Seven Levels of Communication by Michael J. Maher

Our Most Recent Blog

THE POWER OF CREATING OPTIONS

Negotiations and whole life applications

D o you like to negotiate? Some people love it! You probably know someone who is always looking for a deal. Always looking to haggle. And if you have a different perspective, it may seem like they are always looking to argue!

Like it or not, negotiations are a part of life. And just like developing your skills in influence (sales), growth here can really make a difference in your financial success.

Businessman Kevin O'Leary said, "So much of life is negotiation. So even if you're not in business, you have opportunities to practice all around you."

My experience in real estate sales allowed for deep involvement and insight into hundreds of negotiations. I've been able to develop some tactics and strategies, and I've helped numerous deals make it to the closing table. I learned by researching some of the best in the business of negotiations—mainly anyone affiliated with the Harvard Negotiation Project. Then I applied the principles I'd learned to real estate sales and experienced great success along the way.

A few scenarios stand out as exemplary stories. These stories highlight both the principles of negotiations and how to manage your emotions during a deal. These stories also highlight aspects of negotiations that are broadly applicable. As you read these stories, please look for some key principles that will help you strengthen your skills as a negotiator. Lessons include:

1. Stay CALM.
2. Ask great questions and listen!
3. Create options for better decision-making.

In the first story, Jill walked into my office a bit flustered. As one of our top agents and someone who had been performing at a high level for years, being "flustered" was not common for her. She sat down and slid a piece of paper across my desk. "I just wanted to let you know this deal is as good as dead. I am taking this cancellation to the seller for them to sign right now. Buyer already signed."

She started to get up, but I asked her to hold on a moment and sit with me while I digested what she had said. Remember CALM? When things are speeding up around you, sometimes it is best to take a moment and slow them down. Slow down your breathing, let your knee-jerk reactions pass, and take time to develop a deeper understanding. We start the CALM process by first asking questions. *Can you think of a time during a negotiation where you jumped to conclusions before getting all of the necessary information?*

"Tell me more about the situation please," I said.

It turned out the reason she was so concerned about this deal was that there were two other deals contingent upon it happening. In total, these deals represented about $4,000,000 in volume. Jill wasn't worried about herself—she had plenty of other transactions and made excellent money each year. (This is an important mini-lesson. Try not to become too attached to a single outcome. I see newer agents sometimes become so wrapped up in the outcomes of each deal. Why? Because they don't have much else going on! *Part of why we need to create options in negotiations is because the person who has more options generally has more success.*) It turned out, though, that she thought it was a mistake for all parties to let the deal fall apart based on their personal circumstances. But the situation had gotten beyond her influence.

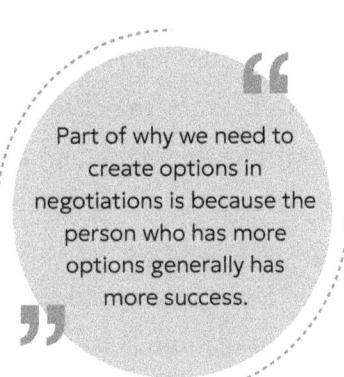

"Why is it falling apart?" I asked. She explained that while the buyer was confident in their ability to borrow the money necessary to close, it was taking longer than expected because the buyer was currently moving and changing jobs. Some lenders are better than others at this. In the process, the buyer had already requested and received from the seller two extensions on their financing contingency period and closing date, and they were now asking for a third. But the seller was having none of it. At this point, the seller felt like they had no control, and to them, the buyer was taking advantage of that. A line was drawn in the sand, and the answer was no. There would be no more extensions. The seller would put the house back on the market.

"Is it the right thing to do?" I asked.

"No. It took us eight months to get it under contract, and there are no other buyers right now. The seller has a contract to purchase a home that's perfect for them, and it's a house that was contested. Plus, there are other buyers lined up. If they cancel that sale, they will most likely lose it."

This was a tough one. I completely understood the seller's position. In a real estate transaction, the seller has most of the leverage under normal markets or seller markets—until the home is under contract. Once that happens, the buyer often has more leverage. Sometimes, buyers can get a little greedy, and the sellers end up feeling like they are being pushed around. *Have you ever been in a negotiation where egos got in the way? Of course! It happens all the time.*

"Let's go meet with the seller," I said.

"It won't do any good. He is adamant."

"We'll see what happens. First, tell me about the seller's personality."

Understanding your audience is a key part of any negotiation or communication. The DISC assessment (Dominant, Intuitive, Sensing, and Compliant) tells us that there are four basic personality types and hundreds of combinations of these types. Most everyone has a dominant preference. After listening to Jill describe the seller, I concluded that we were dealing with a High D—someone who very much likes to be in command, in charge, and whose greatest fear is being taken advantage of. Our job just got a little tougher. *Do you ever stop to think about the personality type you are dealing with when negotiating? It can make a world of difference. You can communicate in a way that is more likely to be well-received.*

At this point in the process, most people would get the feeling they were being taken advantage of at least a little bit. With a High D personality—someone who loves to be in control and whose greatest fear is being taken advantage of—this was a recipe for disaster.

ONE TO GROWN ON

"Here's what we are going to do next. Before we meet the seller, let's speak with the buyer's agent and ask them a couple questions."

We needed to create options. We got the buyer's agent on the phone and asked a couple simple questions. First: How confident is the buyer that they will be able to secure the mortgage? The answer: 100% confident. Second question: If they are so confident, are they willing to put their deposit money on the line? (In this scenario, the buyer was asking for an extension of the time allowed to secure financing. If they were unable to do so, they could cancel the contract and get their deposit money back.) My next question was: If the seller agrees to extend the closing date again, will the buyer be willing to waive off the financing contingency and forfeit their deposit if they are unable to get the loan?

This was a big deal. In many cases, deposit money amounts are in the low thousands. For this deal, there was $50,000 at risk.

And guess what? The buyer agreed! They were so confident they would get the mortgage that they agreed to forfeit their deposit and waive the financing contingency. Now we had options.

We took it one step further. The buyer had already signed a cancellation agreement, so we had them also sign an extension of closing and waiver of financing contingency. We could have just taken the second agreement to the seller and pleaded with him to sign it, but we wanted more. We wanted to be prepared. *Preparation is key here. Think through a situation where you were negotiating with someone who was more prepared than you. How did it go?*

The agent asked me to accompany her to meet with the seller, and I suggested we do it at the seller's home—on their turf. We walked in the door, and introductions were made. After some brief building of rapport, the agent tossed me the ball. First, I asked if we could find a place to all sit down. Mr. Seller suggested his office, and we all walked in. Mr. Seller sat in a big chair behind his big desk, while Mrs. Seller and my agent sat off to the side. I sat across the desk from Mr. Seller in a chair you might find in an elementary school. My knees were literally tucked against my chest. It was a classic High D setup.

See what I did up until that point in our interaction? I kept our rapport brief. If we were dealing with an intuitive personality, a highly social person, I would have spent more time on that step—but High Ds like to cut to the chase. Then I asked Mr. Seller to take us somewhere to sit. My actions had immediately placed Mr. Seller in control.

Next, I apologized on behalf of the buyers for the unfortunate request for another extension. "I know this is frustrating. They are frustrated with the process as well, and we all can only imagine how it feels on your side of the transaction." This created alignment between buyer and seller, whereas before the seller had been more alienated.

"The buyer really wants the home, but he also understands if you need to move on. Sign this document; the buyers already have. We will cancel the deal, release the binder deposit back to the buyer, and put your home back on the market and get ready for more showings."

I handed a copy to Mrs. Seller, who had indicated to me that Mr. Seller would be calling the shots. And then I placed the cancellation in front of Mr. Seller and let that sink in. But not for too long.

"Your other option, if you'd prefer a different direction, is to grant the buyer a closing extension—but not an extension of the financing contingency. That way, should the buyer not close by the new date because of financing, you would receive their deposit money in the amount of $50,000."

ONE TO GROWN ON

I placed the other amendment right next to the cancellation. There was a line that clearly stated something to this effect: "The financing contingency is hereby waived, and the buyer agrees that their deposit money will be forfeited should they not close by X date unless failure to close is the seller's fault."

Who was in the power seat now? You know it. Can you guess the outcome? I bet not.

You see, I expected the seller to sign the extension over the cancellation. I thought it would be a close call based on how angrily the seller initially reacted, but it's what my gut told me nonetheless. Here's what I did not see coming: The seller slid the extension amendment closer to him, read it once more, and **crossed off the part about the buyer forfeiting their deposit.** In other words, Mr. Seller agreed to an extension of closing date AND financing contingency. It was exactly what the buyer had requested to begin with, only this time there was no temper tantrum from the seller.

What had changed? We put the seller in the power seat, which was his comfort zone, and he no longer felt taken advantage of. It was never about seller versus buyer—it was about who was calling the shots. This is a very powerful lesson in life. Whenever people are feeling boxed in, create options for them—especially if you are dealing with D personalities.

To close the story, that deal and the contingent transactions all closed. Think about how many deals in business and life would come together if people were just a little more comfortable negotiating. Sometimes fear of the unknown can cause us to operate in unreasonable ways. Let me see if I can help here with another acronym I created.

Don't be afraid of negotiations. They can be a real PICNIC! This might help you in your next negotiation:

> **P**repare better than the other side: This is the most important step in negotiations.
> **I**dentify common ground: Negotiations that create wins for all also create lasting relationships.
> **C**onfront the challenges, not each other: This reduces stress and points towards a solution.
> **N**egotiate from your strengths: Know your leverage and communicate it.
> **I**solate remaining issues: Breaking disagreements up into smaller parts can make everything less overwhelming.
> **C**lose the matter with clarity: Make sure everyone is on the same page. That way, expectations aren't missed.

To become a better negotiator:

1. Take the DISC assessment to see what personality type you are and to better understand others. You can do so for free on my website www.MomentorsLLC.com.
2. Seek opportunities to practice the PICNIC strategy. Start simple (i.e., by debating where you will eat dinner with friends).
3. Approach negotiations, when possible, with a collaborative mindset.

ONE TO GROWN ON

Negotiating skills are applicable in many moments throughout life. We are constantly negotiating with our friends, family, and ourselves. And that's a fact.

I will say there is a time and a place for tough and direct conversations. If you aren't willing to be direct, you may get taken advantage of. Or worse, you might allow people you are advising to make bad decisions and then have to live with those decisions. If you are an expert in a field and the person you're advising is not, it is important to be able to look them in the eye and say, "You should follow my advice."

> "Negotiating skills are applicable in many moments throughout life. We are constantly negotiating with our friends, family, and ourselves. And that's a fact."

There was one such time when I was advising a friend on real estate. I had his condo listed in Stuart. The year was 2006, and the market had shifted—but not quite to the point where sellers were adjusting their pricing accordingly. We had an offer in hand on this listing for $590,000, which the buyer had communicated was their "highest and best" offer. By the way, that rarely is the case, but in this instance, I felt it was. The seller had paid a price of $750,000 for the unit just one year earlier. So, he found the offer to be insulting and insisted we put it back on the market.

My intuition told me differently. I consulted with my broker, who agreed that things were going to get much worse before they got better.

It took three or four conversations with the seller before he said, "I am now inclined to take the offer." They were difficult conversations, even though this particular person was smarter than most and could have ultimately said no. He eventually took the advice and signed the offer.

He and I kept in touch for a while. I'll never forget what he said one year later. "Kevin, not a day goes by where I don't appreciate the advice you gave me to sign that deal and get rid of that condo." The value one year later? Around $275,000.

Stories don't always end on such a positive note (just think about the buyer of that condo). For instance, in 2007, I helped some folks buy a condo in a different market. At the time, certain economists thought the market had hit rock bottom. The financial crisis of 2008 proved all of us wrong. The folks who owned the condo would have had to hold onto it for quite a while to come out ahead. Ah, if only there had been a crystal ball. Thankfully, people buy real estate for many reasons other than financial gains. This family was looking for a southern vacation home they could enjoy with their family for years to come. At least they got that. We take in information and do the best we can—it's all we can do. Those who study and aim to hone their craft a little each day will be in far better position than those who don't.

Creating options can also lead to better outcomes for you or those you represent. Once, I was negotiating a deal on a home in Sewall's Point as the listing agent on the property. At the time, we were right in the middle of a severe buyer's market. We were the third agents on the listing, which was initially taken at $750,000. When we had the opportunity to interview for the listing, we knew it was now a low $500s deal. We explained this to the seller, who still wanted to list the property at $600,000.

We explained to the seller that $600,000 was an unlikely price, but we would give it a go. We also came to an understanding that we would reduce the price over the course of the next six months on a schedule if it did not sell. I really don't like this strategy because price reductions reduce seller leverage, but it is sometimes necessary.

ONE TO GROWN ON

Especially when the seller has had agents in earlier who set their expectations way too high.

About two months in, the sellers were getting a little agitated. They had just finished a home on the water and had moved, so this empty home was now simply a financial burden to them. They agreed to a price reduction and reduced their asking price to $575,000. And guess what? They got an offer!

For $450,000. That's what we call a "lowball" offer.

There was no negotiating it. The seller countered a couple times, but the buyers wouldn't budge. After a week of back (and no forth), the seller was now considering accepting the offer.

Not so fast. I knew the power of options, and I also knew nothing motivates buyers like other buyers. I needed to try something.

The approach I suggested to the seller was risky. It could have easily backfired, in which case we would've been left with zero offers. But $450,000 was ridiculous in my mind, even in that environment. So I mapped out a plan and the seller agreed to take the risk.

We dropped the price of the home from $575,000 to $550,000, and I scheduled an open house. I advertised the heck out of it. I told the lowball buyer's agent they ought to come by and visit the home again for a second look. That way, they could see if they were willing to go any higher with an offer.

What happened next was amazing. I packed the place with people. We had 30 or so groups visit the open house. The lowball buyers never showed up, but we did get another offer. For $525,000! Did I provide value to the sellers? I had just created a superior selling option for them. They were tripping over themselves to sign the new offer, but for various reasons, I convinced them to counter at $535,000. They were hesitant but did it anyway. And just like that, we had a done deal.

Options are powerful.

The point:

1. Create options for people if they feel boxed in. Especially if you are dealing with High D personalities.
2. Try not to get emotional in business scenarios. Understand that people are different and process things differently.
3. Be willing to have difficult conversations with people. And get face to face when possible. Come from a place of caring, and everything will fall in line. If it doesn't, that's okay too.

Three more to explore:

Beyond Reason by Roger Fisher and Daniel Shapiro
Getting to Yes by Roger Fisher and William Ury
Crucial Conversations by Patterson, Grenny, McMillan, and Switzler

Our Most Recent Blog

GET IT DONE

ROUTINES, NOT RUTS

Change it up to keep it fresh

Let's have some fun.

In a minute. First, a reminder.

Daily habits drive success. There has been quite a bit of space in this book dedicated to habits, and even a few suggestions to consider. Hopefully you have implemented some new habits along the way. If not, now would be the time to start. There is very little downside to developing good habits and eliminating bad ones. The only thing is—your routines might start to feel like ruts. Master the mundane and you might be super successful, but there are some things you can do along the way to keep the process fresh and enjoyable.

You see, growth happens outside of our comfort zones. All significant growth. The biggest wins you have achieved in life came through after a period of fear, challenge, and struggle. This includes learning to walk, ride a bike, or swim, earning your first seven-figure income,

> "Master the mundane and you might be super successful, but there are some things you can do along the way to keep the process fresh and enjoyable."

or stepping up to your first public speaking engagement. After you develop great habits, the habits become more comfortable. To continue to stretch and grow, we must expand our scope or improve upon those habits and find new things to take on and conquer. This will give us creativity and fuel to improve our routines. It also ensures our lives don't stagnate.

Let's have some fun and look at ways to prevent your routines from turning into ruts—ways to expand your horizons, grow, and flourish. The key is to try new things. When appropriate, including spouses, friends, and family can make many of the below even more fun. It is important also to keep some of these lessons just for yourself. You decide! Let's use the acronym FORBES as a model.

The F in FORBES is for **Family and Friendships**. Other than your faith journey, what could be more important? Our habits and routines can interfere here if we aren't intentional about investing time into these important relationships. Here is a list of possible actions to take to change it up with the people closest to you—and to develop new relationships along the way:

<u>Family and Friends</u>

- Meet up with someone for a morning walk or join a running club or fitness group.
- Embrace random acts of kindness through writing personal notes, texts, and sending gratitude videos.
- Smile, stop, and talk with someone you normally would pass right by.
- If you see a social media post where someone is struggling, call them instead of commenting online.

- Offer to mentor someone in an area you have great expertise in.
- Respond to social media posts by lifting people up and congratulating them.
- Handwrite personal notes to people who would least expect it.
- Help your significant other with additional chores around the home.
- Help a neighbor in need (offer a hand carrying groceries, doing yardwork, etc.).

The O is for **Occupation**. It represents whatever you do for a living. If you love what you do, you may find it naturally uplifting to show up every day and do the work. But often, work can become a grind. Switching things up when possible will help us give our job our best daily and help others do the same:

Occupation

- Get a certification relevant to your career.
- Make it a point to ask really good questions every day. And listen to the answers!
- Drive a new way to and from work (this is admittedly random, but it can help you break out of your rut).
- Change up your workspace.
- Start the side gig you've been putting off by taking one small step in the right direction.
- Read a new book about your industry.
- Pay someone at work a direct and specific compliment.

- Pay someone an indirect compliment by telling their boss or their friend how awesome they are.

The R is for **Recreation**. It includes your hobbies and interests—things you do for fun. If you are doing the same things over and over again, perhaps some new endeavors are what the doctor ordered:

Recreation

- Make a list of things to do related to your interests that you've never done before. Try to check one off each week. (Have an indoor list for rainy/cold days and an outdoor list to get nature's benefits.)
- Take lessons for a musical instrument to increase your skills and improve brain function.
- Watch an informational program or documentary on a subject that interests you.
- Turn off the 24-hour news nonsense. 30 minutes a day is plenty. (And that might even be too much!)
- Take an art class.
- Eat at a new restaurant and pretend you are a food critic. Post your "analysis" to social media.
- Cook something for dinner that you've never made before.
- Watch a classic movie you've never seen.
- Try a new sport.
- Play a board game you have never played.
- Listen to a new music station every week to expand your horizons—go beyond the "popular" stations.

- Travel somewhere you've never been and immerse yourself in local customs and food.
- Start a garden.
- Paint your room a different color.
- Sing out loud. And sing often!

B is for **Body and Health**. What are you doing to stay fit? How is your nutrition? Do you have an exercise routine? This is where things can really turn into ruts. We must keep looking for new ways to keep our body and mind healthy:

Body and health (consult your doctor first)

- Change up your exercise program, jog a different route, or add weight training to the mix. Try swimming, biking, or hiking.
- Dance to your favorite music for five minutes before starting your work for the day.
- Join a program that is right for you—F45, Orange Theory, CrossFit, etc.
- Switch up your morning positive reading to include different authors. Read outside of your comfort zone! Maybe include a podcast as well.
- Try to incorporate new, nutritious whole foods and healthy beverages into your diet.

E is for **Education and Personal Growth**. What are you doing to make sure you aren't just going through the motions and getting older? What are you doing to develop in areas outside of your normal work and routines? Here are some ideas:

Education and Personal Growth

- Take a class at a local university or select an online option.
- Learn a new language.
- Connect with someone in your family or at work you haven't developed a relationship with yet.
- Read a book or magazine about an industry other than yours that interests you.
- Read a fiction book for fun and to learn about varying points of view and perspectives. Then read some non-fiction!
- Practice to become a great story-teller.
- Start writing in a journal.
- Find a new podcast.
- Change up your affirmations every 45 days (or after you start seeing results in your current area of work).
- Join the One To Grow On online community.

S is for **Spirituality**. This part is very personal. Here are a couple of my thoughts, but you should certainly add some to make this section your own:

Spirituality

- Create or follow a prescribed Bible reading plan and follow it each day.

- There are many books written on different types of meditation. Read those books and then try a few variations.
- Find a worthy cause that makes your heart sing. Donate money and time to it.
- Share your gratitudes with a gratitude partner. Or write them in a journal!
- Pray.

Get after it:

1. Pick one of the examples in this chapter that you do not currently do, and then do it this week. Just one! Write it down.

The point:

1. Good habits performed consistently can lead to a great life.
2. Good habits that become boring and mundane can become *too* comfortable. To keep growing and improving, it is necessary to change things up and stretch.

KEVIN M. WAUGAMAN

Our Most Recent Blog

CONCLUSION

Use the STAIRS!

I appreciate you investing in and reading this book—but there are no congratulations in store for simply finishing it! Reading this book does very little for you unless there has been a seed planted in you that germinates now or in the future. You must have an enhanced mindset and take action. I would like to hear from you if you took action after reading this book or if you developed a new and improved mindset and you find it's benefited you in leading a strong, fulfilling life. Visit www.MomentorsLLC.com and send me a note. Or sign up for our newsletter to continue your growth journey!

Your thoughts are a reflection of your past experiences, your inputs, your mentors, and what you listen to. Your beliefs are a reflection of what inputs you value most and of your self-talk. You must take action, which is why I have given you dozens of suggestions throughout this book. Nothing happens without action.

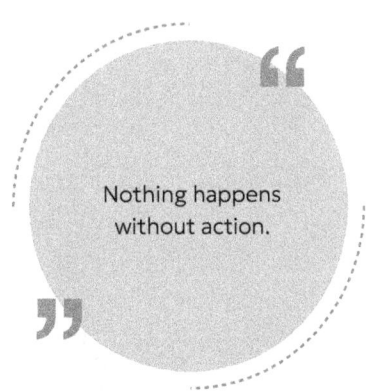

"Nothing happens without action.

When John Maxwell spoke to our team at Berkshire Hathaway HomeServices Florida Network Realty, he described a process he uses to implement new things. It went something like this:

- Test
- Learn
- Adjust
- Reenter

I expanded on this a bit and once again created an acronym to help me remember it. I give the credit to Maxwell; I simply made it more memorable *for me and you*. I call it the STAIR process:

Start – Take action on something (a first step).

Track – Pay attention to the process and note the results.

Analyze – Think through your steps. Are the results in line with your time and/or monetary investment?

Improve – Adjust your approach, attitude, and activities as needed.

Refocus – Take the next action based on your evaluation.

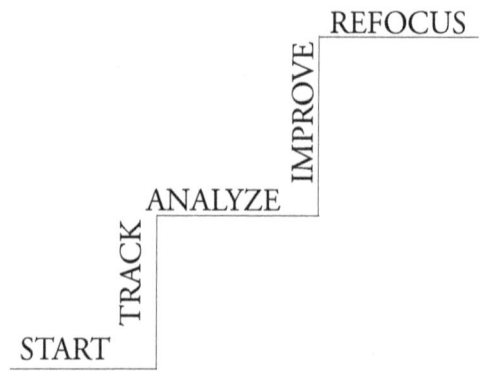

ONE TO GROWN ON

The beauty of this acronym is that as repeat this process over and over, you will be climbing the STAIRs on your journey toward your dream!

There will be stumbles along the way.

Learn from yesterday, then be done with it.

Have hope and vision for the future, then attach action to it.

The real focus is on today. Focus on that first step. Then focus on the next step. Even if you don't know the steps that come next, at least you're focused on your goals!

Okay. That's it. I leave you with this short chapter on taking action. Invest the time you would have spent reading a longer chapter on taking action. Take a step forward.

Go. Do. Don't overthink it. Live!

Take steps consistently and you will achieve at a level beyond your expectations.

As coach Dan Devine said in the brilliant movie *Rudy* (which you should watch if you haven't already), "You already know this, but this is the most important game of your lives. No excuses—do the work."

I hope this experience for you was truly One To Grow On.

APPENDICES

From "Flock With the Right Crew" chapter.

Grandpa: Make a game out of anything.
Grammy: Set a good example in how you live.
Grandaddy: Pay attention to the details.
Nanny: Make learning fun.
Marina: Follow Jesus.
Donna: Laugh, LOUD!
Shirley: Love your family.
Clay: Be courageous.
DJ: Show up and be present.
Dave B: Make others feel special—because they *are* special.
Dave M: Prioritize what matters most.
Steve: Be a presence.
Ric: Care deeply for others and show it.
Brian: Don't take things personally.
Ron: Be warm and kind to others.
Raji: Lead with your heart.

KEVIN M. WAUGAMAN

Values Photograph

WAUGAMAN FAMILY VALUES

Jesus Christ is our Lord and Savior!

WE ARE UNIQUELY AND WONDERFULLY MADE IN HIS IMAGE

WE LOVE EACH OTHER AND SHOW IT

WE REFLECT GOD'S LIGHT
WE ARE LIFELONG LEARNERS
WE ARE A TEAM

We appreciate everything He provides us

WE ARE HONEST WITH OURSELVES AND OTHERS

WE TAKE ACTION — WE ARE DOERS — WE GET IT DONE

We can learn something from everyone

WE PRAY
WE LAUGH WITH EACH OTHER AND ENJOY MAKING PEOPLE SMILE

WE LEARN FROM MISTAKES TO GROW IN WISDOM

We are good stewards of our abundance

WE INTENTIONALLY ADD VALUE TO OTHERS EACH DAY

ONE TO GROWN ON

Other affirmation examples:

I love Jessica sacrificially and unconditionally, and show it.
I am a strong father who nurtures our children.
I am a lifelong learner through books and experiences.
I am healthier each day, growing in energy and my passion for life.
I am intentional with my time and present in the moment with the people around me.
I am a great connector with people and of people.
I inspire people and instill confidence.
I am a best-selling author impacting millions of lives in a positive way.
I am a sought-after coach and speaker who unlocks potential and clears obstacles for clients.
I am a leading real estate executive at the top of my game.
I care deeply for others and look for ways to add value.
I am a world traveler and am interested in other cultures.
I am a great listener and have a strong memory.

Recommended For Further Reading

Title	Author	Subject
10% Happier	Dan Harris	Living Life
34 Forever Agent Proclamations	Allan Dalton	Sales
7 Habits of Highly Effective People	Stephen R. Covey	Habits

Title	Author	Subject
8 Ways to Support Diversity, Equity, and Inclusion for All	Johnnie Johnson and Dr. Michael E. Webber	Executive
America The Last Best Hope	William J. Bennett	History
American Creation	Joseph J. Ellis	History
Atomic Habits	James Clear	Habits
Awakened Imagination	Neville Goddard	Mindset
Be a People Person	John C. Maxwell	Relationships
Benjamin Franklin	Walter Isaacson	History
Beyond Reason	Roger Fisher/ Daniel Shapiro	Negotiations
Blue Ocean Strategy	W. Chan Kim/Renee Mauborgne	Competing
Buffett: The Making of an American Capitalist	Roger Lowenstein	Finance/ Investing
Change Your World	John C Maxwell	Mindset
Conscious Coaching	Brett Bartholomew	Coaching
Courage is Calling	Ryan Holiday	Mindset
Crucial Conversations	Patterson/ Grenny/ McMillan/ Switzler	Negotiations
Decision Points	George W. Bush	History
Developing the Leader Within You	John C. Maxwell	Leadership
Discipline Equals Freedom	Jocko Willink	Execution
Elite	Nick Hays	Leadership

Title	Author	Subject
Emotional Intelligence 2.0	Travis Bradberry/ Jean Greaves	Mindset
Every Moment Matters	John O'Sullivan	Coaching
Everyday Greatness	Stephen R. Covey	Character
Everyone Communicates Few Connect	John C. Maxwell	Relationships
Execution	Larry Bossidy and Ram Charan	Execution
Extreme Ownership	Jocko Willink/ Leif Babin	Leadership
Find Your Why	Simon Sinek	Marketing
George Washington's Secret Six	Brian Kilmeade	History
Get Out of Your Own Way	Dave Hollis	Success
Getting to Yes	Roger Fisher/ William Ury	Negotiations
God's Armor Bearer	Terry Nance	Faith
Good to Great	Jim Collins	Execution
Great By Choice	Jim Collins	Execution
Green Light Selling for the 21st Century	Don Aspromonte	Sales
Hard Optimism	Price Pritchett, Ph.D.	Mindset
Heavy Hitter Sales Linguistics	Steve W. Martin	Sales
Holy Moments	Matthew Kelly	Spirituality
How to Develop Self-Confidece and Influence People by Public Speaking	Dale Carnegie	Public Speaking

Title	Author	Subject
How to list and Sell Real Estate	Danielle Kennedy	Sales
How to Stop Worrying and Start Living	Dale Carnegie	Living Life
How to Win Friends and Influence People	Dale Carnegie	Relationships
If the Tomb is Empty	Joby Martin	Faith
Influence	Robert B. Cialdini	Psychology
Intentional Living	John C. Maxwell	Living Life
Interviewing More Than a Gut Feeling	Richard Deems	Management
Killing Kennedy	Bill O'Reilly	History
Killing Lincoln	Bill O'Reilly	History
Killing Reagan	Bill O'Reilly	History
Know What You're For	Jeff Henderson	Marketing
Lead Like Reagan	Dan Quiggle	Leadership
Leaders Eat Last	Simon Sinek	Leadership
Leadershift	John C. Maxwell	Leadership
Leadership 101	John C. Maxwell	Leadership
Leadership and the One Minute Manager	Ken Blanchard	Leadership
Leadership Isn't for Cowards	Mike Staver	Leadership
Leading in Tough Times	John C. Maxwell	Leadership
Life's Gretest Lessons	Hal Urban	Living Life
Lighter	Yung Pueblo	Mindset
Make the Impossible Possible	Bill Strickland	Success
Managing the Whirlwind	Michael Annison	Management
Man's Search For Meaning	Viktor E. Frankl	Mindset

ONE TO GROWN ON

Title	Author	Subject
Mastering the Art of Selling Real Estate	Tom Hopkins	Sales
Mindset	Carol S. Dweck	Mindset
More Than a Carpenter	Josh McDowell/ Sean McDowell	Faith
Negotiation	Harvard Business Essentials	Negotiations
Nine Minutes on Monday	James Robbins	Execution
Ninja Selling	Larry Kendall	Sales
Power of Awareness	Neville Goddard	Mindset
Predictably Irrational	Dan Ariely	Psychology
Quiet	Susan Cain	Personality Types
Rainmaking Conversations	Mike Shultz	Sales
Raving Fans	Ken Blanchard	Sales
Rich Habits	Thomas C. Corley	Habits
Secrets of the Millionaire Mind	T. Harv Eker	Success
Smart Talk	Lou Tice	Mindset
Sometimes You Win Sometimes You Learn	John C. Maxwell	Success
Start With Why	Simon Sinek	Marketing
Starting a Business	Walter Grant	Start Up
Steve Jobs	Walter Isaacson	Success
StrengthsFinder 2.0	Tom Rath	Personality Types
Talk Like Ted	Carmine Gallo	Public Speaking
Team of Rivals The Political Genius of Abraham Lincoln	Doris Kearns Goodwin	History

Title	Author	Subject
The 10-Minute Energy Solution	Jon Gordon	Mindset
The 15 Invaluable Laws of Growth	John C. Maxwell	Success
The 21 Irrefutable Laws of Leadership	John C. Maxwell	Leadership
The 36-Hour Day	Nancy Mace and Peter Rabins	Health
The 360 Degree Leader	John C. Maxwell	Leadership
The 3G Way: Dream, People, and Culture	Francisco S. Homem de Mello	Leadership
The 4 Disciplines of Execution	Chris McChesney/ Sean Covey/ Jim Huling	Execution
The 8th Habit	Stephen R. Covey	Habits
The Advantage	Patrick Lencioni	Execution
The Answer	John Assaraf and Murray Smith	Mindset
The Automatic Millionaire Homeowner	David Bach	Finance/ Investing
The Book of Forgiving	Desmond Tutu/ Mpho Tutu	Mindset
The Case for Christ	Lee Strobel	Faith
The Compound Effect	Darren Hardy	Habits
The Difference Maker	John C. Maxwell	Mindset
The Divine Mentor	Wayne Cordeiro	Faith
The Energy Bus	Jon Gordon	Mindset
The Four Agreements	Don Miguel Ruiz	Character

ONE TO GROWN ON

Title	Author	Subject
The Go-Giver	Bob Burg and John David Mann	Character
The Happiness Advantage	Shawn Achor	Mindset
The Intelligent Investor	Benjamin Graham	Finance/Investing
The Inventor's Bible	Ronald Louis Docie, Sr.	Invention
The Law of Divine Compensation	Marianne Williamson	Mindset
The Leadership Challenge	James M. Kouzes/Barry Z. Posner	Leadership
The Leadership Handbook	John C. Maxwell	Leadership
The Lessons of History	Will and Ariel Durant	History
The Little Red Book of Selling	Jeffrey Gitomer	Sales
The Miracle Morning for Real Estate Agents	Hal Elrod/Michael Maher/Michael Reese	Habits
The Nuclear Effect	Scott Oldford	Start Up
The One Minute Manager	Ken Blanchard	Leadership
The Power of a Positive Team	Jon Gordon	Teamwork
The Power of Awareness	Neville Goddard	Mindset
The Power of Full Engagement	Jim Loehr/Tony Shwartz	Habits
The Power of Intention	Dr. Wayne W. Dyer	Mindset

Title	Author	Subject
The Psychology of Money	Morgan Housel	Finance/Investing
The Ride of a Lifetime	Robert Iger	Leadership
The Seven Levles of Communication	Michael J. Maher	Sales
The Slide Edge	Jeff Olson	Habits
The Speed of Trust	Stephen M.R. Covey	Character
The Steve Jobs Way	Jay Elliot	Success
The Ten Stories Great Leaders Tell	Paul Smith	Leadership
The Thinker's Edge	John C. Maxwell	Mindset
The Toyota Way	Jeffrey K. Liker	Execution
The Untethered Soul	Michael A. Singer	Spirituality
The Upside of Irrationality	Dan Ariely	Psychology
The Warren Buffett Portfolio	Robert G. Hafstrom	Finance/Investing
Think and Grow Rich	Napoleon Hill	Mindset
Think Like a Freak	Steven D. Levitt/Stephen J. Dubner	Mindset
Thomas Jefferson The Art of Power	Jon Meachem	History
Time Management from the Inside Out	Julie Morgenstern	Time Management
Today Matters	John C. Maxwell	Habits
Trump: The Art of the Deal	Donald Trump	Negotiations
Tuesdays With Morrie	Mitch Albom	Living Life
Unlimited Power	Tony Robbins	Mindset

Title	Author	Subject
What Got You Here Won't Get You There	Marshall Goldsmith	Success
What It Takes	Stephen A. Schwarzman	Leadership
Why We Want You to Be Rich	Donald Trump/ Robert Kiyosaki	Success
Win the Day	Mark Batterson	Mindset
Winning With People	John C. Maxwell	Leadership
Worthy	Jamie Kern Lima	Mindset
You Are a Badass	Jen Sincero	Mindset
You Are a Badass at Making Money	Jen Sincero	Success
Your 1st Year in Real Estate	Dirk Zeller	Sales
Your Brain Is Always Listening	Daniel G. Amen, MD	Health

www.ingramcontent.com/pod-product-compliance
Lightning Source LLC
Chambersburg PA
CBHW030729150426
42813CB00051B/354